Jacques C. Mbongue

How
I
See God:
What About You?

2

Preface

Our perception of God is deeply personal yet profoundly impactful. It shapes our understanding of the divine, influences our relationship with the sacred, and provides us with a compass for navigating the complexities of life. The human perception of God is a subject of endless fascination, a tapestry woven by the diverse experiences, beliefs, and journeys of individuals throughout history.

The Bible, serving as the fundamental source for any theological framework, encompasses a collection of profound narratives that illuminate the experiences of men and women who encountered God in extraordinary ways. These encounters manifested through various means, including divine revelations, intimate personal interactions, and the ongoing development of a lifelong relationship with the Divine. It is through these stories that we glean invaluable insights into the profound nature of God's involvement in the lives of individuals throughout history.

However, it is important to acknowledge that the Bible represents a fraction of the vast tapestry of God's interaction with humanity. While it provides a rich and inspired account of divine encounters, it does not exhaust the infinite ways in which God can reveal Himself to us. God, being boundless in His resources and wisdom, continually unveils new dimensions of His character, His love, and His purpose to those who seek Him earnestly.

This 27-chapter devotional book invites you on a reflective and soul-stirring exploration of the human perception of God. It is a compilation of contemplative insights and heartfelt poetic writings that seek to delve into the depths of our understanding, connection, and encounters with the Lord. Through these pages, we embark on a journey that transcends cultural boundaries, encourages diverse perspectives, and seeks to find common threads that unite us in our quest for spiritual truth and meaning.

The chapters within this book are not intended to provide definitive answers or impose a singular perspective of God. Instead, they serve as gentle guides, encouraging introspection, fostering dialogue, and inviting the reader to embark on their own personal odyssey of faith. Each chapter offers a unique lens through which we can explore chronologically the rich tapestry of human experience in the Bible and the ways in which our perceptions of God shape our lives, relationships, and purpose.

As you immerse yourself in these pages, you will encounter stories of triumph and struggle, moments of awe and doubt, and glimpses of divine presence in the ordinary and extraordinary moments of Scriptures and my life. You will hear the voices of seekers, believers, skeptics, and above all, humans in the biblical context, all contributing their insights and reflections on the infinite facets of the divine-human relationship.

This book does not seek to diminish the mystery and transcendence of God, nor does it claim to capture the entirety of divine essence within its pages. Rather, through my humble eyes and life experiences offers an opportunity to ponder, question, and contemplate the depth of our connection with God. It acknowledges the limitations of human perception while celebrating the boundless capacity of the human spirit to long for a meaningful relationship and a profound encounter with the Creator.

May this devotional book serve as a source of inspiration, comfort, and spiritual nourishment on your own unique journey of perception, belief, and relationship with God. May it ignite within you a renewed sense of wonder, a deepened appreciation for the sacred in everyday life, and a greater understanding of the diverse ways in which humanity perceives and experiences God.

In the pages that follow, we embark together on a sacred pilgrimage of the heart, exploring the boundless depths of human perception and the transformative power of encountering God.

May you find inspiration, and spiritual enrichment within these pages.

With heartfelt blessings,

Jacques C. Mbongue, PhD

Acknowledgements

I would like to express my deepest gratitude to my beloved wife, Yanne, whose unwavering support, encouragement, and love were instrumental in the creation of this book. Your unwavering faith and dedication to seeking the face of God have inspired me to dig deeper into the Scriptures, and your insightful perspectives have enriched the content of these pages. Thank you for being my constant companion on this spiritual journey.

To my precious daughters, Welly, and Amalia, you are my greatest joy and inspiration. Your innocent hearts and boundless curiosity remind me of the wonder and awe that lie at the heart of our perception of God. Your presence fills my life with immeasurable blessings, and I am grateful for the light you bring into my world.

I would also like to extend my heartfelt appreciation to Pastor David Lee for his invaluable insights and guidance throughout the process of writing this book. Your wisdom, knowledge, and genuine passion for God's Word have truly enriched the depth and understanding conveyed in these pages. Your thoughtful feedback and encouragement have been indispensable, and I am profoundly grateful for your mentorship.

Lastly, I humbly acknowledge the divine presence that permeates every aspect of this book. To God, who reintroduced Himself to me with overwhelming grace and love, I am eternally grateful. Your presence in my life, your divine guidance, and the countless moments of revelation have fueled the words written on these pages. May this book be a testament to your unfailing love and an offering of gratitude for the transformative power of encountering You.

In closing, I extend my deepest appreciation to all who have played a part in bringing this book to fruition. Those through your constant promptings, your unwavering support, prayers, and belief in my vision have been a source of immense encouragement. May the words contained within these pages ignite hearts, deepen faith, and illuminate the path to a profound encounter with the divine presence.

With heartfelt gratitude,

Jacques Mbongue, PhD

Table of Contents

Preface

Chapter 1: It's Only the Beginning

Chapter 2: Divine Anesthesia

Chapter 3: Where are You?

Chapter 4: Loving the Enemy

Chapter 5: A Jealous God

Chapter 6: Would You Move for Me?

Chapter 7: I Heard the Cry You didn't Utter

Chapter 8: What is Your Name?

Chapter 9: "What is That in Your Hand?"

Chapter 10: When He Believes in You

Chapter 11: Why is it so Hard?

Chapter 12: The Last-minute Rescue God

Chapter 13: The Beauty of Holiness

Chapter 14: Trust the Process

Chapter 15: Worship Me

Chapter 16: A Faithful God

Chapter 17: An Eternal God

Chapter 18: It's Just a Test

Chapter 19: A Lover of Praise

Chapter 20: An Unwavering Word

Chapter 21: A God in Love with Darkness

Chapter 22: A Still Small Voice

Chapter 23: A Heart Easily Touched by Prayer

Chapter 24: A Know-it-all God

Chapter 25: "So, you think you can God?"

Chapter 26: Not Pressed by Time

Chapter 27: An Unchanging God

1. It's Only the Beginning

In the beginning God created the heavens and the earth. The earth was without form, and void; and darkness was on the face of the deep. And the Spirit of God was hovering over the face of the waters. Then God said, "Let there be light"; and there was light.
Genesis 1:1-3

Let's take our minds to this very moment when creation was to begin. The most striking event that often goes unnoticed is the presence of God at the very beginning. The word "beginning" generally refers to the start or origin of something. It can describe the initial stage or point in time when something starts to exist or happen. In a broader sense, "beginning" can also refer to the underlying principles or foundation upon which something is built or established.

In many contexts, "beginning" carries a sense of importance and significance, as it represents a fresh start, a new opportunity, or a turning point. For example, the beginning of a new year is often seen as a time for reflection and setting goals, while the beginning of a new chapter in one's life may involve significant changes or challenges. *"In the beginning God..."* is written first to remind us that there is only a beginning because of *Who* is in it. How encouraging it is to know that at the very start there was Someone so powerful about to bring everything into being!

My next thought goes to what comes next. *"The earth was without form, and void; and darkness was on the face of the deep. And the Spirit of God was hovering over the face of the waters."* In the biblical account, the earth was *"without form and void,"* and darkness covered the surface of the deep. Some scholars interpret this to mean that the earth was a formless, watery mass that was yet to be molded into its current shape. Others see it as a metaphor for a world without order or purpose, waiting to be transformed by the creative power of God. Regardless of the interpretation, the phrase *"without form"* suggests a state of disarray or incompleteness, awaiting the intervention of a divine force to bring order and meaning to the universe.

What captivates my attention the most is the contrasting imagery presented in the description of the chaotic state of the earth, where everything seems disordered and devoid of hope. The term "hovering" suggests a gentle movement, like a bird brooding over its nest, indicating the imminent creative action of God. The Spirit's presence signifies the divine life-giving power that would transform the formless void into a beautifully ordered creation. Amidst this disarray, there is a profound revelation that the Spirit of God was actively present, gently hovering over the surface of the waters, seemingly undisturbed by the chaos. It is intriguing to contemplate why the Spirit of such an omnipotent, beautiful yet Holy Being would engage with an environment characterized by disorder and despair. The answer lies in the intention of showcasing His immense creativity. He happily chooses to engage with and bring forth transformation in situations marked by lowliness, hopelessness, discouragement, melancholy, dejection, loss, grief, despondency, or despair. This very principle is exemplified in the life of Jesus Christ, who, in order to fulfill the powerful plan of salvation, willingly entered a world plagued by disease and death, offering a stark contrast and the promise of redemption. He remains undeterred by the depths of our darkest imaginations, unfazed by the lowest points we perceive ourselves to reach.

How frequently have we found ourselves trapped in seemingly hopeless situations with no apparent way out? Undoubtedly, many times. Yet, it is crucial to acknowledge that God possesses unparalleled expertise in bringing forth something out of nothing. He excels in the remarkable artistry of crafting beauty from the ugly, restorations from the ashes and life from death. With the profound simplicity of four words, "let there be light," what was once shrouded in obscurity became illuminated with exquisite clarity and splendor. Darkness yielded to the radiance of illumination, as beams of light pierced through the void. In that remarkable moment, creation sparked life, unveiling a tapestry of colors, shapes, and forms. Shadows receded, unveiling the beauty and intricacy of the world.

The experience of nothingness can also arise when we perceive our present circumstances as unchangeable, devoid of any conceivable solutions or escape routes. God employs a distinct approach to lead us to acknowledge the insurmountable nature of our problems, so that when He unveils His power, we are filled with awe and astonishment. He delights in that awe-inspired gaze, for it signifies our trust in His ability to overcome other seemingly impossible situations as well. Standing at the edge of the vast and tumultuous Red Sea, with the thunderous hooves of thousands of horses closing in from behind, hope seemed utterly lost. The Israelites were on the verge of returning to a life of slavery, and the fear of brutal retaliation for the Egyptians' firstborns being struck down by their God loomed over them, threatening the lives of their own children. In that pivotal moment, God orchestrated a phenomenon that defied scientific explanation, as the Red Sea miraculously parted to create a path for an entire nation to cross. Amidst this incredible event, the lives of the fish peacefully continued in the depths of the divided waters, an entire people crossed on a dry sea floor while the pursuing Egyptian army met its fate as the sea closed upon them, returning to its natural state.

I would like to stress this. God flourishes in the realm of humanly impossible, defying the boundaries and limitations that confine our understanding. In the face of what seems insurmountable to us, God's power and purpose emerge with unrivaled strength and unwavering determination. He orchestrates the extraordinary out of the ordinary, the miraculous out of the mundane. When we reach our limits, God's boundless capabilities are revealed, showcasing His sovereignty over all circumstances and His ability to accomplish what is deemed impossible by human standards.

If you experience loneliness, it is in His presence that loneliness finds its purpose. If you feel a sense of emptiness, that free space within you is there by design. It is for Him to fill it up with Himself: *"So do not fear, for I am with you; do not be dismayed, for I am your God. I will strengthen you and help you; I will uphold you with my righteous right hand."* **Isaiah 41:10**. He takes pleasure in creating dwellings in the wilderness, especially when we find ourselves in such places. He also revels in leading us to such desolate places, sometimes when our maladive over-inflated sense of self-worth leads us to believe there is no other way than our own. He also and mainly leads us to the wilderness because it's only in its nothingness that the totality of His transformative and creative power can be manifested. When we reach a point where there is no one else to whom we can turn but the One who has performed the marvelous works, our only option is to offer Him the glory. Thus, induced loneliness should not be resented or resisted. It should be viewed as a reset button, one designed to restore God to His proper place in our lives. God sees loneliness as an invitation to experience His presence, find companionship and grow in our relationship with Him.

When we find ourselves feeling misunderstood, it is an opportunity for God to become our ultimate sounding board. He is able to fully comprehend the intricacies of our emotions, even when we ourselves struggle to understand them. There are no secrets or mysteries about our feelings that escape His knowledge. He invites us to pour out our hearts to Him, to express our deepest thoughts and emotions without fear of being taken out of context. In His presence, we are seen and understood completely. God's perfect understanding of our innermost being allows Him to provide the guidance we need. He is the One who truly comprehends the depths of our hearts and desires to walk with us through every season of life.

Frequently, we find ourselves questioning whether God cares, where He is, and why good people experience hardship. We yearn for justice and seek answers. Yet, we must remember that there is no task too difficult for Him, and His wisdom never falters. The truth is, He is present, right there, hovering over the surface, ready to bring about a transformative change and turn everything on its head. The most remarkable works of the Creator often commence from a state of apparent chaotic mess. Even if you thought you were at the end with no signs of hope in sight, rest assured that you are not. Embrace the journey ahead, for it is only the beginning, filled with untold possibilities!

The Beginning of it All

In the depths of eternity's embrace,
Where time and space first found their place,
In the dawn of creation's wondrous birth,
God stood tall, the Author of the Earth.

Before the cosmos adorned the skies,
Before the sun began to rise,
In that sacred moment, pure and true,
God's presence shone, forever new.

He spoke, and galaxies came to be,
With celestial wonders, vast and free,
With every breath, He formed the stars,
Crafting beauty from afar.

In the stillness of the cosmic sea,
God's voice whispered, "Let there be."
From darkness sprang a brilliant light,
Illuminating the depths of night.

He fashioned oceans, mountains, and land,
With divine artistry, His touch so grand,

From swirling clouds to gentle breeze,
Every element is shaped with perfect ease.

And in this wondrous symphony,
God wove a thread of eternity,
For He, the Creator, was present there,
Breathing life into the open air.

Through the ages, His love remains,
A steadfast beacon that never wanes,
From the beginning, until the end,
God's presence, our eternal friend.

He guides us with His loving hand,
Through every season, we understand,
That in each moment, big or small,
God is there, embracing all.

So let us marvel at His creation's might,
And bask in the glory of His light,
For in the beginning, and evermore,
God's love and presence we adore.
Yours Truly

"I am the LORD, your Holy One, The Creator of Israel, your King." Thus says the LORD, who makes a way in the sea and a path through the mighty waters. **Isaiah 43:15-16**

2. Divine Anesthesia

> *And the Lord God caused a deep sleep to fall on Adam, and he slept; and He took one of his ribs and closed up the flesh in its place. Then the rib which the Lord God had taken from man He made into a woman, and He brought her to the man. And Adam said: "This is now bone of my bones. And flesh of my flesh. She shall be called Woman because she was taken out of Man." Therefore, a man shall leave his father and mother and be joined to his wife, and they shall become one flesh.* **Genesis 2: 21-25**

Anesthesia is often needed for medical procedures that would otherwise cause significant pain or discomfort to the patient. Its primary goal is to induce a temporary loss of sensation or consciousness, so that the patient does not feel pain or discomfort during the procedure. There are different types of anesthesia that can be used depending on the nature of the procedure and the patient's individual needs. For example, local anesthesia may be used to numb a specific area of the body, while regional anesthesia may be used to numb a larger region such as an arm or a leg. General anesthesia, which involves putting the patient into a state of unconsciousness, may be used for more complex procedures or surgeries.

In Genesis 1:21-25 there is a strikingly similar procedure that God Himself performed. By causing a deep sleep to fall on Adam, He was able to perform a surgical act aimed at presenting him the most beautiful gift he's ever received outside of his own life, his woman! While reading this beautiful story, I can't help but wonder why putting Adam to sleep was necessary. Why couldn't he witness the creation of the person that will stand by him for the rest of his life? The answer lies in the result. He loved it!

"And the Lord God caused a deep sleep to fall on Adam, and he slept". God induced a profound slumber in Adam, but it was up to Adam to surrender to sleep. For God's perfect purpose to unfold in our lives, we must also learn to sleep. Resisting slumber would mean not trusting God's watchful care and relying on our own consciousness, logic, and control. When we depend solely on our own sense of reason, we are more susceptible to doubt and anger because many of the experiences we encounter may not align with our understanding or logic. When we fail to trust in God's love and omnipotence, we may miss out on the wondrous outcomes of His divine plan. It is for our own benefit to enter into a peaceful slumber of trust. It's best for us not to seek to understand the process, and the less we do, the better it gets! I mean, imagine Eve! God made Adam, but Eve made a poet!

The process leading to God's purpose for our lives may not always make sense to us. I'd like to think of us like small arthropods walking on a gigantic portrait painting. We may aimlessly roam around the portrait for years but later find out we were only walking around the representation of an "eye" of the painting, when there was a lot more to gaze upon. We will never see the big picture! God who spoke light and everything that exists into being, could have spoken Eve, into existence as well. Yet, He chose to go the surgeon route. The most exquisite blessings that God has prepared for us do not necessitate our active involvement or vigilant control. This is exactly why we must fully trust Him by going to sleep. No debate or questions. It is worth it.

"Being awake" could also hurt. Imagine Adam being fully conscious of his rib cage being ripped open. He would have probably wondered why the God that just made him a few moments ago would want to tear him apart now! How traumatic that could have been for him! He could single-handedly have aborted the making of his biggest blessing by fighting back. The reason why we often see God as a mindless monster, with the sole intention of ruining our lives, taking away the people we love or leading us through the most difficult circumstances could simply be because we found ourselves wide awake during the surgery that will produce our "Eve". We were supposed to be under anesthesia!

One might wonder how we can be awake and go to sleep at the same time. The answer is found in **Proverbs 3:5-6:** *"Trust in the Lord with all your heart And lean not on your own understanding; In all your ways acknowledge Him, And He shall direct your paths."* The Bible does not promote the idea of us becoming mindless beings, abandoning our intellect completely. Instead, we are encouraged to acknowledge our limitations and place our complete trust in God, recognizing that our understanding is limited, and His wisdom far surpasses ours.

Let's consider all the times we have decided to have control over everything that takes place in our lives. How much has the micromanagement of our existence cost us our health and peace? In today's world, many of us depend on anxiolytics to cope with the uncertainties of life because the desire to have a sense of control over tomorrow can be overwhelming. This can lead to a constant state of fear and unease. This fear often arises from our reluctance to embrace restful sleep in God's wisdom and love. Let's go to sleep!

The First Marriage

As slumber's embrace released its hold,
Adam awoke, his eyes unfold.
From dust he came, a creation pure,
To find a world of wonder, so secure.

With drowsy eyes, he saw the light,
A radiant beauty, a mesmerizing sight.
Eve, formed by God's loving hand,
Stood before him, on this sacred land.

In awe he beheld her graceful form,
A companion chosen, his heart warm.
Her presence ignited a flame within,
A love story destined to begin.

He marveled at her tender grace,
A reflection of God's loving embrace.
Her eyes sparkled with a gentle glow,
A garden of love, beginning to grow.

Adam's heart soared with joy untold,
As Eve's beauty he did behold.
Their souls connected, destinies entwined,
A union blessed, forever aligned.

Together they embarked on life's grand stage,
Exploring creation with boundless rage.
Hand in hand, they walked in unity,
Bound by love's eternal divinity.

In Eden's embrace, love's song unfurled,
As Adam and Eve embraced their world.
A story of love's sweetest bliss,

A divine union, sealed with a kiss.

Yours Truly

"For My thoughts are not your thoughts,
Nor are your ways My ways," says the Lord.
For as the heavens are higher than the earth,
So are My ways higher than your ways,
And My thoughts than your thoughts."- **Isaiah 55:8-9**

3. Where are You?

And they heard the sound of the Lord God walking in the garden in the cool of the day, and Adam and his wife hid themselves from the presence of the Lord God among the trees of the garden. Then the Lord God called to Adam and said to him, "Where are you?"
Genesis 3:8-9

Imagine walking home alone at night, the darkness engulfing your surroundings. Suddenly, you become aware of the sound of footsteps echoing behind you. Your heart skips a beat as you turn around, only to see a mysterious figure sprinting towards you. Fear courses through your veins as you realize they are chasing you. Your instinct compels you to run, but with each stride, your legs grow heavier, impeding your escape. Glancing over your shoulder, you witness the figure closing in, their breath hauntingly close. You attempt to cry out for help, but your voice fails you, suffocated by fear. Panic takes hold, and a sense of desperation engulfs you as you desperately try to outpace your pursuer. *"Trees! Quick let's hide!"* You gasp. Thoughts of the unknown assailant's intentions torment your mind. Will they inflict harm upon you? Will anyone come to your rescue in time? With every passing moment, your terror intensifies, and the nightmare-like reality of the situation becomes inescapable.

What did I just describe? I couldn't be possibly talking about the good and loving God of the Universe chasing Adam and Even in the garden! Yet, this is what they felt after they've disobeyed. God suddenly made them shudder and vainly hide in the daylight among the shadows of the trees He Himself made from the sound of his voice. Surprisingly, this promptly made Him ask: *"Where are you"*?

Someone might ask you "*where are you?*" when they want to know your current location or whereabouts. This could happen in a variety of situations, such as:

If you are meeting someone in person and they are trying to locate you. God respects the set time of meeting with you. He is consistently punctual. It is conceivable that during the *"cool of day"*, He would regularly rendezvous with His recently created children and cherished companions. He eagerly anticipated those encounters, filled with anticipation. Regrettably, they opted to partake in a pointless game of "hide and seek" with a God who possesses the unwavering ability to always locate them.

If you are lost or have become separated from a group of people, and they are trying to find you. Sin acts as a profound divide between us and God, not only on a spiritual level but also in our physical existence. What makes it tragic is that we often remain unaware of our deviation from the right path. Sin can be likened to a speeding vehicle that carries our unaware selves away from home, while deceiving us into thinking that have never left. When God asks, "Where are you?" it is not because He has lost sight of us, but to help us realize the extent to which we have strayed. Adam and Eve, in their shame, sought refuge behind trees, attempting to hide from the One who sees through all things. Where were they? They sought solace in their own distorted perception of safety, losing sight of God as their true refuge. How frequently do we build makeshift fortresses out of our own intellectual constructs? In our quest to bask in the glory of our perceived accomplishments, it is all too easy to forget that our achievements did not originate solely from within ourselves. We often overlook the fact that we are not the sole architects of our successes. There exists a greater force, a divine presence that guides and influences our paths, bestowing upon us the opportunities and abilities to achieve greatness. With the advancements of science and technology today, we may erroneously perceive ourselves as self-sufficient and independent from our Creator, capable of creating our own sense of security. Yet such efforts prove as futile as attempting to conceal ourselves from the Almighty behind a cluster of mango trees.

If the person is trying to coordinate plans with you and needs to know your location in order to make arrangements. God is an actively seeking God. It is truly uplifting to realize that God will persistently search for us, even when we try to hide in what appears to be secure and hidden locations. He remains eager to engage with us and plan, despite our repeated failures to keep our commitments. For God, *"being out of sight"* does not mean *"being out mind"*. No matter what transgressions we may have committed, all He desires is to spend time with us, akin to a loyal companion. His love for us is unwavering, and nothing can sever that bond. Shall we continue to conceal ourselves under the burden of guilt and shame? Such an endeavor is futile.

Where are you?

In the garden, where life first bloomed,
God sought His creation, Adam, presumed,
With gentle steps and knowing grace,
He wandered through that sacred space.

His voice, like a whisper in the breeze,
Called out to Adam among the trees,
"Where are you, my beloved one?
Come, let us commune beneath the sun."

Through foliage green and petals fair,
God's search continued, with tender care,
He knew the hiding place Adam had found,
But sought to draw him from the ground.

In the quiet of that hallowed ground,
God's footsteps echoed, gentle sound,
His eyes, filled with love and longing,
Searched for Adam, weak and wandering.

He found him hiding, filled with shame,
Cloaked in guilt, bearing the blame,
But God, in His mercy, drew near,
With compassion to calm Adam's fear.

"Adam, where are you?" He gently asked,
Knowing the answer, the soul unmasked,
Yet with a heart of love, unyielding,
He called Adam forth, His presence revealing.

Adam emerged, eyes downcast and low,
Feeling the weight of his choices, the woe,
But God's forgiveness, like a healing balm,
Restored his heart, bringing peace and calm.

For though Adam had strayed, lost his way,
God's relentless love would never sway,
He sought him out, to reconcile,
To bring redemption, to make him smile.

In that encounter, in the garden's embrace,
God's love and grace filled every space,
For He seeks us all, with open arms,
To bring us back to His loving charms.

So when we wander, feeling alone,
Remember God's pursuit, how He's known,
He looks for us with unending grace,
To bring us back to His warm embrace.
Yours Truly

"For thus says the Lord God: "Indeed I Myself will search for My sheep and seek them out." - **Ezekiel 34:11**

4. Loving the Enemy

And Cain said to the Lord, "My punishment is greater than I can bear! Surely You have driven me out this day from the face of the ground; I shall be hidden from Your face; I shall be a fugitive and a vagabond on the earth, and it will happen that anyone who finds me will kill me." And the Lord said to him, "Therefore, whoever kills Cain, vengeance shall be taken on him sevenfold." And the Lord set a mark on Cain, lest anyone finding him should kill him. **Genesis 4: 13-15**

There is a peculiar allure to things that pose eventual harm, even though we are aware of the risks involved. It's intriguing how foods rich in sodium and cholesterol, despite being detrimental to our health, often boast the most delightful flavors. Similarly, I find it fascinating that God shares a similar connection with the people He loves. Even though we might bring Him significant sorrow, He remains a steadfast presence, diligently watching over us and granting us each new day as if we are indebted to Him. I am simply unable to comprehend the boundless love God has for individuals who do not reciprocate it or who seemingly merit the full weight of His justice.

Malignant jealousy led Cain to kill his brother and instead of feeling any sort of remorse, he became arrogant. *"I do not know. Am I my brother's keeper*? He replied to the question God asked *"Where is Abel your brother*? **Genesis 4:9**. Again, God did not ask this to inquire where Abel was. He did so Cain would realize what he had done. Yet, he didn't even seem to care. God continued patiently, as if to persistently help Cain realize the gravity of his actions. *"What have you done? The voice of your brother's blood cries out to Me from the ground."* **Genesis 4:10.** Seeing this did not help Cain understand the impact of his actions, the Lord tried a new astute approach: present him with the consequences! *"So now you are cursed from the earth, which has opened its mouth to receive your brother's blood from your hand. When you till the ground, it shall no longer yield its strength to you. A fugitive and a vagabond you shall be on the earth."* **Genesis 4:11-12.** In His incommensurable love, God must have thought, *"perhaps this would bring him back to me"*.

To this, Cain immediately responded but seemed only concerned with the fallout. *"I shall be fugitive and a vagabond... and whoever find me would kill me."* To this, many of us on the outside would say out loud, *"that's exactly what you get"* or *"you'd better be glad you're not dead."* That's because, truthfully that's pretty brazen of him to say, especially after displaying unashamed haughtiness. This request was devoid of any remorse. It was instead laden with dreadful anxiety.

What is most astonishing in this story is not the request itself, but God's response to it. He declares, "*...whoever kills Cain, vengeance shall be taken on him sevenfold.*" God takes it upon Himself to protect Cain from anyone seeking to commit the same crime against him. In fact, He issues a warning that His punishment would be seven times more severe for anyone who dares to harm Cain. This insight offers a profound glimpse into the character of God. His judgment carries a perfect balance of justice and grace. While the spilled blood would bring consequences upon the ground, no one was to take Cain's life. It reveals that we serve a God who even responds to a plea devoid of any remorse. If God showed such responsiveness to the anxious thoughts of a remorseless murderer concerning his own life, how much more would He listen to our pleas for forgiveness and respond to our other worries and fears?

Only a few judges would reduce the impact of a sentence solely based on the plea of the offender. It is difficult for us to comprehend the significance of this story because we often overlook the fact that even those who cause us great harm are deeply loved by God, just as we are. Are we okay with God loving our enemies? As God posed the question to Jonah, one cannot help but consider: Are humans not more valuable than vines? Could it not be possible that God holds a similar level of emotion and concern for the city of Nineveh, an evil and vast population lost in their way? The book concludes with God seeking Jonah's permission to extend His mercy to His enemies. This is the character of God. A God more interested in love and forgiveness than vengeance. We should, therefore, reflect upon whether our desires for harm to befall those who have wronged us are truly aligned with God's intentions for us and for them. It is crucial to examine whether these wishes stem from the depths of our own evil hearts rather than being in accordance with God's divine plan for our lives.

In **Acts 13:22**, David is referred to as "*a man after [God's] own heart,*" prompting me to contemplate the significance of this statement. I realized that God and David shared certain similarities: both had a son who did not harbor affection for his father. Absalom,

King David's third son, embarked on a covert mission to undermine his father's rule due to his pride. Scripture portrays Absalom as exceptionally handsome and flawless in appearance. He assumed the role of a judge in Jerusalem and made grand promises about what he would do if he were king. This scheme persisted for years until Absalom requested to go to Hebron, where he orchestrated his own proclamation as king (**2 Samuel 13**).

Upon his entrance into Jerusalem as the proclaimed king, Absalom sought to consolidate his power by seizing David's house and engaging in intimate relations with his concubines—an act deemed unforgivable. Astonishingly, David refrained from participating in any retaliatory actions against his son. Instead, he explicitly instructed his generals to show kindness and mercy towards Absalom, despite his treason. Scripture emphasizes that David's orders regarding Absalom were heard by all the troops. However, these orders were disregarded, and the generals acted contrary to David's command. David mourned deeply over his son, to the extent that it profoundly affected the morale of the army. Their victory felt hollow, and they returned to the capital in shame rather than triumph. Despite the deep betrayal and disobedience from Absalom, David's love for his son remained unwavering. It demonstrates the complexity of the relationship between a father and his child, mirroring the enduring love and compassion that God has for His people, even in the face of their transgressions.

Indeed, there is a parallel between the account of David and Absalom and the relationship between God and His son, Satan. Prior to his fall, Satan was described as a beautiful and powerful creature, possibly the most prominent among the angels (**Ezekiel 28:12–13**). He was even referred to as the "guardian cherub," indicating his role in God's presence. However, pride led to Satan's downfall. Instead of acknowledging God as the source of his exalted status, Satan took pride in himself, leading to his rebellion against God. Similar to how David lamented over Absalom, God also instructed Ezekiel to raise a lamentation over the king of Tyre, symbolizing Lucifer as he fell from heaven. Just as Absalom wreaked havoc in David's kingdom, Satan causes chaos and evil in the world, manifesting as violence, disease, and death. Despite this rebellion, God has chosen not to retaliate against Satan in a destructive manner yet. As seen above, the scriptures suggest that God will even lament over the destruction of His fiercest enemy as he is destroyed, just as David mourned his son Absalom who meant no good to him. The unfathomable love that God demonstrates even towards His enemies is a concept beyond human comprehension. It is this very love that calls us to love our own enemies, as stated in **Matthew 5:43-48**. To truly love and experience God in our lives, we must extend love even to those who cause us pain.

The profound love and forgiveness demonstrated by God serve as a powerful example for us to follow. When we encounter situations that seem unforgivable, it is essential for us to strive to cultivate forgiveness. Just as God's love transcends the gravity of the most abhorrent crimes, and the nature of the most hardened criminals, we should not hold onto self-destructive grudges against our fellow human beings. By embracing forgiveness, we acknowledge the transformative power of love and demonstrate our understanding of the boundless capacity for growth and redemption. Holding onto grudges not only harms our relationships with others but also takes a toll on our own well-being. Just as we are called to forgive others, we must also learn to extend that same compassion and forgiveness to ourselves. In mirroring God's love and forgiveness, we can break free from the cycle of resentment and self-destruction. Letting go of grudges allows us to experience inner healing, cultivate healthier relationships, and create an atmosphere of compassion and understanding. It is through forgiveness that we open ourselves to the fullness of love and embrace the transformative power of God's grace.

Blessed is he whose transgression is forgiven,

Whose sin is covered.

Blessed is the man to whom the Lord does not impute iniquity,

And in whose spirit there is no deceit. --- **Psalm 32:1-2**

Cain's Poem

After a murder, in Cain's heart, darkness crept,
A burden he carried, a secret he kept.
"My punishment," he cried, "is more than I bear,
Banished from Your presence, burdened with despair.

Cast out from the land, I'll wander and roam,
A fugitive, a vagabond, no place to call home.
Hidden from Your face, forever lost I'll be,
And those who find me, shall surely seek to slay me."

But the Lord, in His mercy, heard Cain's plea,

And placed a mark upon him, for all to see.
A sign of protection, a shield in his plight,
Preserving his life, through day and through night.

For vengeance, the Lord proclaimed, on those who dare,
To harm Cain, sevenfold their punishment they'll bear.
A mark of distinction, a grace undeserved,
A testament of God's mercy, unswerving and reserved.

In Cain's poem, we glimpse the weight of the lack of guilt,
The consequences he faced, the remorse he did not build.
A haunting reminder of sin's bitter cost,
And the mercy of God, even for the lost.

Let us reflect on Cain's tale, with introspection,
And ponder the choices that lead to his rejection.
For in his story, we find a cautionary plea,
To heed God's voice and choose His path faithfully.

May we learn from Cain's plea, so profound,
To seek redemption, on Mercy's solid ground.
To turn from sin, and in God's protection dwell,
Finding forgiveness and salvation, breaking the spell.

Cain's poem speaks of consequences untold,
Yet within it, God's mercy unfolds.
A reminder that even in our darkest strife,
There's hope and redemption, through God's eternal life.
Yours Truly

5. A Jealous God

And they said, "Come, let us build ourselves a city, and a tower whose top is in the heavens; let us make a name for ourselves, lest we be scattered abroad over the face of the whole earth." But the Lord came down to see the city and the tower which the sons of men had built. And the Lord said, "Indeed the people are one and they all have one language, and this is what they begin to do; now nothing that they propose to do will be withheld from them. Come, let Us go down and there confuse their language, that they may not understand one another's speech." So, the Lord scattered them abroad from there over the face of all the earth, and they ceased building the city. **Genesis 11: 4-8**

A planned uprising against God was initiated by humanity, who constructed a city to prevent their dispersion across the entire earth. This act was one of rebellion and defiance, as they built a towering structure to attain fame and recognition. These types of structures, which aspire to reach great heights, are commonly referred to as "skyscrapers." The concept behind this tower was to construct a monument that would rise high into the heavens.

The goal was to avoid being scattered throughout the earth, which directly contradicts God's command in **Genesis 9:1**. This act of uniting against God's command demonstrates human arrogance and wickedness, as evidenced using Babel and Babylon as symbols of organized human rebellion throughout the Bible. In fact, in Revelation, Babylon is referred to as the "mother of harlots" and the "abominations of the earth" (Rev 17:5), representing the organized defiance of God that occurs in the last days in which we live.

According to current historical and archaeological evidence, it is believed that the Tower of Babel was located at Eridu in Mesopotamia. The structure of the tower was most likely in the form of a multistoried Ziggurat, which was similar to a pyramid or ancient temple. Ziggurats were considered by worshipers to be sacred mountains that the gods descended upon to reach the earth. Symbolic sacred mountains played a vital role in most pagan religions in ancient times. In the ancient Near East, both ziggurats and natural mountains were believed to be the dwelling places of the gods. They were regarded as the meeting point between heaven and earth, where gods met humanity. The ziggurat was perceived as the center of the cosmos, and it was the physical means for humans and gods to make direct contact with each other. In general, the Bible associates tall towers with human arrogance, as seen in Isaiah 2:12-15, 30:25, and Ezekiel 26:4,9.

Indeed, at the center of this enterprise is arrogant and defiant pride, meddled with distrust of God. Indeed, He promised the earth would never be destroyed by water again. They must have thought, *"if we all take refuge on tower that touches heaven, there could be survivors on the next flood."* How many times have we taken things in our hands because we were dubitative of God's intentions and doubtful of His promises?

Seeking unity against God is the most devastating pursuit we can embark upon. When we unite in doing evil, we become our weakest, far inferior to the strength we possess when we rely solely on the Lord. Our feeble attempts cannot compare to God's intentional desire to save us from our own destructive tendencies, even in this era of perceived intellectual prowess. Sometimes to save us from ourselves, God may come and scatter everything we've built out of self-reliance and self-confidence. The confidence that we ought to have had in God, but instead put in ourselves and others, will be mocked by chaos and disillusion. The result will be an abandoned building now at the mercy of erosion and winds. What a waste of resources!

God's relentless pursuit of bringing us back to Him knows no bounds. Like a loving and desperate father longing for His children, He will go to great lengths to seek and find us, no matter where we may be. He will exert every effort to rescue us from the self-imposed traps and challenges we find ourselves in. His persistent calling will resound ceaselessly until we make the choice to respond and return to Him. Patiently, He will wait for us at the door of reconciliation, eagerly anticipating our homecoming. In His infinite love, He may even allow circumstances that wound us, not out of cruelty, but for the purpose of bringing about our ultimate healing and restoration. God's unwavering commitment to reconcile with us is a testament to His boundless love and grace.

God's passion for the honor and reverence due to Him is unwavering, and He has little tolerance for idolatry. As the Almighty, He rightfully expects to be the sole object of worship and devotion. The worship of false gods or the creation of idols is a direct affront to His divine authority and supremacy. *"For I, the Lord your God, am a jealous God, visiting the iniquity of the fathers upon the children to the third and fourth generations of those who hate Me."* **Exodus 20:5.** The word "jealous" is translated from the Hebrew word *"Qanna"* (kan-naw') which means literally, "jealous, or zealous". It has been used in the Bible, specifically in Old Testament 6 times and was first used in **Exodus 20:5**. The fundamental essence of this concept is rooted in the metaphor of a marital relationship. In this metaphor, God is depicted as the husband of Israel. He is portrayed as a jealous God who desires exclusive praise and worship from His people, refusing to share His honor and glory with any other, including graven images. This divine jealousy is fierce and intense, often resulting in righteous anger and severe consequences.

Reacting with intense anger when discovering a spouse's infidelity can have tragic consequences for both individuals involved. However, human jealousy is flawed because it relies on the notion of rightful ownership, which extends beyond the bounds of marriage itself. Merely being married to someone does not grant ownership over them. It is worth questioning how we can claim ownership over anything when we don't even have full control over our own existence. It is evident that all glory and creation belong exclusively to God, as there is no other being like Him. Therefore, any response to idolatry or spiritual adultery that opposes God's will is highly displeasing and offensive to Him.

Yet, even amidst God's fervent passion for His honor and the intolerance towards idolatry and self-worship, His love is manifested in what may appear as intrusive interventions. It is in these moments that His deep care and concern for His people shine through. His interventions may involve penetrating into the depths of our lives, exposing our vulnerabilities and shortcomings.

He made them filled with confusion and began speaking in different tongues, creating a language barrier that made it challenging for them to collaborate and work together. He's so in love with each of these rebellious fellows that He thought confusing them with each other would bring each of them back to worshipping Him. This was because no matter what language they spoke, He would understand it. This was because if they feel misunderstood, or unheard, He will stand ready to decipher the complexity of their newly acquired idioms. He would be their confidant, and their friend. Besides, what's the need of building a tower that reaches the heavens when He could live among them?

Where can I go from Your Spirit?

Or where can I flee from Your presence?

If I ascend into heaven, You are there;

If I make my bed in]hell, behold, You are there.

If I take the wings of the morning,

And dwell in the uttermost parts of the sea,

Even there Your hand shall lead me,

And Your right hand shall hold me. -- **Psalm 139:7-10**

6. Would You Move for Me?

Now the Lord had said to Abram: "Get out of your country, from your family And from your father's house, To a land that I will show you. I will make you a great nation; I will bless you and make your name great; And you shall be a blessing. I will bless those who bless you, And I will curse him who curses you; And in you all the families of the earth shall be blessed." **Genesis 12: 1-3**

Abram resided with his family in the land of Chaldea, his place of birth, for a number of years (**Genesis 11:31**). Chaldea was located in Mesopotamia, in what is now modern-day Iraq. It was known for its fertile land, which allowed for successful agriculture, and its location near major trade routes. The people of Chaldea were skilled in various crafts, such as metalworking and weaving, and they were also known for their advancements in astronomy and mathematics. Religion played an important role in Chaldean culture, with a pantheon of gods and goddesses worshiped by the people.

Living in a particular place for one's entire life can have both positive and negative effects on an individual. On the one hand, it can provide a sense of familiarity and comfort as one grows accustomed to the environment and the people in it. One can develop a strong sense of community and belonging, as well as a deep knowledge of the local customs and traditions.

On the other hand, living in one place for a long time can also lead to a lack of exposure to new experiences and ideas. This can result in a narrow perspective and an inability to adapt to new situations. Additionally, it can create a feeling of stagnation and a lack of motivation to explore beyond familiar surroundings. Ultimately, the experience of living in one place for a lifetime depends on the individual and their personal preferences and experiences.

To truly engage in a relationship with God, we must embrace growth, and growth necessitates stepping out of our comfort zones and becoming familiar with new ways. Walking alongside God inherently involves change and change hurts. We cannot expect to remain unchanged once we encounter Him. Each experience we share with Him will push us towards becoming our best selves.

Furthermore, just like in any meaningful relationship, exclusivity becomes an implicit expectation, requiring us to be emotionally faithful to our partner. In order to fully experience God, we need an environment that nurtures an intimate walk with Him. We must be willing to let go of anything that hinders a wholehearted commitment if we desire a deep relationship with Him. God values exclusivity in His relationships.

Furthermore, walking alongside the Almighty God is an expansive and transformative journey that transcends narrow perspectives. In this remarkable expedition, we discover the power of forgiveness for the seemingly unforgivable, the capacity to love those deemed unlovable, and the ability to find serenity amidst life's tempests. These invaluable qualities cannot be acquired through a limited viewpoint but necessitate a multifaceted approach to existence. We acquire them by stepping out of the confines of our own mindset and prideful preconceptions, which often serve as our personal territories. Yes, "getting out of our countries" also entails acknowledging our limited understanding and humbly surrendering acquired knowledge for the wisdom of the All-Knowing. It involves wholeheartedly submitting ourselves to the divine guidance of God.

He will unveil the path we are to traverse. The journey alongside God does not come with a predetermined itinerary. Our sole responsibility is to embark on the journey, without concern for the destination, as long as He is leading the way. Not only does He possess superior knowledge, but He has also pledged to bestow blessings upon us. Let us set forth with conviction and purpose!

"Now it shall come to pass, if you diligently obey the voice of the LORD your God, to observe carefully all His commandments which I command you today, that the LORD your God will set you high above all nations of the earth." - **Deuteronomy 28:1**

7. I Heard the Cry You Didn't Utter

And God heard the voice of the lad. Then the angel of God called to Hagar out of heaven, and said to her, "What ails you, Hagar? Fear not, for God has heard the voice of the lad where he is. Arise, lift up the lad and hold him with your hand, for I will make him a great nation. **Genesis 21: 17-18**

Hagar was a slave woman who was given to Abraham by his wife Sarah in order to bear a child for him. As a slave woman, Hagar suddenly saw in her son's Ishmael the wealth she's never had. He was her future, her insurance policy. As the mother of Abraham's first son, Hagar held an important position in the family. However, after Sarah gave birth to her own son, Isaac, she became jealous of Hagar and Ishmael and demanded that Abraham send Hagar and Ishmael away, and Abraham complied.

Hagar and her son Ishmael were forced to leave Abraham's household and wander in the wilderness of Beersheba. They had only a skin of water and some food with them. As they journeyed, their water supply ran out and they became lost in the wilderness. Hagar, being a devoted mother, became distressed and began to weep. Ishmael, who was a young boy at the time, also became very thirsty and started to cry. In her despair, Hagar placed Ishmael under a bush and went a short distance away, unable to watch her son die of thirst.

What a harrowing scene! Imagine a mother who was once considered insignificant in society but was suddenly bestowed with a level of importance she never imagined she could attain. All of this to witness the treasure of her life waste away from thirst! Picture someone once filled with life and health, wasting away from terminal cancer, or someone else once happy, now riddled with depression and thoughts of suicide. How many times were we on the verge of watching ourselves die?

Despite Ishmael being her everything, Hagar had lost all hope for him and was resigned to essentially closing her eyes to avoid watching him die. Do we also sometimes lose hope for ourselves in seemingly hopeless situations? Though we've all heard stories of courageous individuals fighting with everything they've got against the ravages of disease, I've known many people lose that battle at the very day of the diagnosis. I've known people give up their dreams once they hit a roadblock. I've seen students give up studying from the very first bad test scores.

Sometimes we just don't have the power to fight.

The good news is, even if we don't have the power to continue, the cry we did not utter will be heard. *"What ails you, Hagar? Fear not, for God has heard the voice of the lad where he is."* She yearned for God to rescue her son, yet despair consumed her heart, leaving her feeling utterly hopeless. How comforting it is to know that even our weakest and unspoken pleas will be presented before God, and they will be heard! In times when we feel too weak to fight or express ourselves, the attentiveness of the Almighty God will magnify exponentially to listen to the prayers of our troubles, the cries we could not voice.

Let's thus be encouraged to keep fighting in faith as He hears, listens and cares.

He Cares

In the desert's vast and desolate expanse,
Where scorching and fiery sunbeams dance,
A child's cry pierces through the stillness,
Echoing in the barrenness, the voice of witness.

Ishmael, son of Hagar, his flowing tears cascade,
In the wilderness, his searing pain displayed,
His innocent voice, a plea for relief,
Seeking solace, longing for belief.

Amidst the dunes, where hope seems lost,
Where sands conceal, emotions tossed,
God's ear inclines to Ishmael's cries,
His compassionate heart never denies.

For God, in His infinite love and care,
Listens carefully to every prayer,
No plea goes unheard, no voice unseen,
In the desert's silence, God's presence keen.

With tender grace, God draws near,
Wiping away each falling tear,
Embracing Ishmael in His arms so wide,
Whispering comfort, walking by his side.

In the wilderness, a promise blooms,
God's merciful hand forever looms,
He assures Ishmael of a future bright,
A nation blessed, in His guiding light.

So, when we face deserts of despair,
When cries escape us, burdens we bear,
Remember Ishmael's tale of divine grace,
That God hears our cries in every place.

In the depths of our struggles and strife,
God's compassion reaches into our life,
He listens, He cares, His love remains,
In the desert's trials, His presence sustains.
Yours Truly
"Can a woman forget her nursing child,
And not have compassion on the son of her womb?
Surely, they may forget,
Yet I will not forget you.
See, I have inscribed you on the palms of My hands;
Your walls are continually before Me." --- **Isaiah 49:15-16**

8. What is His Name?

Then Moses said to God, "Indeed, when I come to the children of Israel and say to them, 'The God of your fathers has sent me to you,' and they say to me, 'What is His name?' what shall I say to them?" And God said to Moses, "I AM WHO I AM." And He said, "Thus you shall say to the children of Israel, 'I AM has sent me to you.
Exodus 3: 13-14

A name is a word or set of words that serves as a means of identification of a person, animal, place, thing, or concept. It is a label that is given to an individual at birth or later in life, and it is used to refer to them in conversation, writing, or other forms of communication. From a human perspective, everyone or thing should have a name.

Moses was sent on a mission to speak to the enslaved children of Israel about a God that frees from slavery. He was immediately struck with an internal dilemma. These people don't even know Him! They knew all the of the Egyptian gods and were told to worship them, and now there's another God they had to be introduced to?

Life in slavery was harsh and oppressive. As descendants of Jacob, who had settled in Egypt during a time of famine, they initially found refuge and provision. However, over time, the rulers of Egypt grew fearful of their increasing numbers and began to subject them to bondage and cruel oppression. They were forced into laborious tasks, such as building cities and working in the fields, under the watchful eyes of taskmasters. The work was grueling, and they were treated as mere property rather than human beings with dignity and rights. Their days were filled with exhaustion and despair as they toiled under the scorching sun, enduring physical and emotional abuse. They had little control over their own lives and were subject to the whims and demands of their Egyptian masters. The oppressive nature of their slavery left them with little hope for a better future. Moreover, their oppressors sought to suppress their cultural identity and religious beliefs. The Israelites were forbidden from practicing their own customs and were compelled to adopt Egyptian ways. This attempted assimilation further deepened their sense of loss, alienation, and the longing for freedom.

The Egyptian pantheon consisted of a vast array of gods and goddesses who were worshipped throughout ancient Egypt. Some of the most well-known deities include Ra, the sun god who was seen as the king of the gods; Osiris, god of the afterlife and fertility; Isis, goddess of magic and motherhood; Horus, god of the sky and war; and Anubis, god of embalming and the dead. Each deity had their own unique characteristics, symbols, and mythology, which were often interwoven with one another. Each of these gods had a name, which is why Moses had to aptly ask indirectly the Lord: *"What is your name"*?

To that God answers: ***I AM WHO I AM***. In Hebrew, the phrase is *"ehyeh asher ehyeh,"* which can also be translated as *"I will be what I will be."*

The phrase is significant because it emphasizes the eternal, self-existing nature of God. It suggests that God is not limited or defined by anything outside of Himself, but rather exists independently and unchangeably. It also implies that God is the source of all existence and the one who sustains all things. God does not need a name like the Egyptian sun god or the god of the dead. *"I AM WHO I AM"* emphasizes that God is the one who defines Himself and is not subject to the definitions or limitations of human beings. His name is a statement of God's transcendence and holiness, and a reminder that He is beyond human understanding and comprehension.

"*I am*" in the English language is a statement of existence, indicating that the speaker or subject of the sentence exists. From a human perspective, though we use it to describe our own existence, it is used with an inherent fatal flaw because though *we are* today, *we may not be* in the future. Despite our finite nature caused by sin, humans describe their existence in a similar manner to God because He has placed eternity in our hearts and are made in His image. (**Ecclesiastes 3:11** and **Genesis 1:26**). Therefore, when God says, *"Thus you shall say to the children of Israel, 'I AM has sent me to you."* It has the compelling authority of eternity imbedded in it. If *"I AM"* has sent me, *"I AM"* will be there when I arrive and will be there when I depart. Decades, centuries and millennia liquefy before *"I AM"*. *"I AM"* will forever be there and has the power to deliver you from the hands of the slave masters. There is no richer name that exists in the entire universe. This is the name of our Creator.

He was yesterday, He is today and will be tomorrow and for eternity. What He says is trustworthy. What an unchanging rock He is! In His name alone was the assurance the entire people of Israel needed. They did not need a description of Him like all the other Egyptian gods depend on to be identified. He could remain invisible and command the power of His Being just by the sound of His name. That's power.

Some trust in chariots, and some in horses;

But we will remember the name of the Lord our God.

They have bowed down and fallen;

But we have risen and stand upright. --- **Psalm 20:7-8**

9. "What is that in Your Hand?"

> *Then Moses answered and said, "But suppose they will not believe me or listen to my voice; suppose they say, 'The Lord has not appeared to you.' So, the Lord said to him, "What is that in your hand?" He said, "A rod." And He said, "Cast it on the ground." So, he cast it on the ground, and it became a serpent; and Moses fled from it. Then the Lord said to Moses, "Reach out your hand and take it by the tail" (and he reached out his hand and caught it, and it became a rod in his hand), "that they may believe that the Lord God of their fathers, the God of Abraham, the God of Isaac, and the God of Jacob, has appeared to you."* **Exodus 4: 1-5**

On the previous chapter we've seen how God answered Moses to a question regarding His name. Though powerfully compelling as it was, Moses still had some questions about how the Israelites would receive him. *"But suppose they will not believe me or listen to my voice; suppose they say, 'The Lord has not appeared to you.'* Moses indirectly showed his lack of faith in God's promise to free his people, expressed through concerns about being rejected. It seems ironic since he was conversing with a bush on fire that did not burn, why would he doubt that God could make his own messenger persuasive?

We often as Christians have no problem believing in the power of God. We just have a hard time believing He would do what He has said. What we forget is that God's very power resides precisely in His capacity to back up what He says. If God were to say, "*Let there be light*" and the light hesitated or only provided a faint glimmer out of politeness or disobedience, what would we think of Him? He would not be considered God! Thus, to believe in the power of the God of the Universe while doubting His Word and promises is inherently insulting.

However, when Moses asked that question, God responded with patience and began with a teaching moment. He asked Moses, "*What is that in your hand?*" before addressing his concerns. This approach demonstrated that God is always willing to work with tangible things we hold dear before building faith which pertains to the unknown. Rods were used to prevent people from stumbling while walking independently on rocky terrain. Moses held a rod in his hand, which symbolizes the control humans desire over their lives without God's intervention. It symbolized self-assurance and independence. It is comparable to the money in our bank accounts or the careers and relationships we have that make us feel secure.

Yet, in a moment's notice, all of these things can be stripped away, leaving us with no choice but to rely on a helping hand. God invited Moses to let go of his control by ordering him to cast his rod on the ground because He wanted to show him that it was neither his appearance nor his gift of gab that would make him successful in his mission, but God's power alone. When we surrender our desire to micromanage our lives, and hold on to the control we desire, we open ourselves up to supernatural experiences and miraculous living. By releasing our grip, we will witness the amazing things God had intended for us all along, while we were busy trying to manipulate the outcome of our own plans.

After Moses realized that his perception of reality was incorrect- with the rod turning into a snake- he had to place his complete trust in God. This meant following God's command to pick up his rod by its tail. Occasionally, it may require witnessing and undergoing unimaginable occurrences to have complete faith in God. However, it is not part of God's plan to let us learn through difficult experiences. Our task is to have complete faith in His unsurpassed ability to fulfill His promises.

Moses gained a newfound confidence in himself and his mission once he fully realized that he the Lord of Hosts was in command. Similarly, we can also live our lives with confidence and child-like assurance knowing that the Almighty God has complete control over the outcome of our existence.

Trust in the Lord with all your heart,

And lean not on your own understanding.

In all your ways acknowledge Him,

And He shall direct your paths. -- **Proverbs 3:5-6**

10. When He Believes in You

Then Moses said to the Lord, "O my Lord, I am not eloquent, neither before nor since You have spoken to Your servant; but I am slow of speech and slow of tongue." So, the Lord said to him, "Who has made man's mouth? Or who makes the mute, the deaf, the seeing, or the blind? Have not I, the Lord? Now therefore, go, and I will be with your mouth and teach you what you shall say." But he said, "O my Lord, please send by the hand of whomever else You may send." So, the anger of the Lord was kindled against Moses, and He said: "Is not Aaron the Levite your brother? I know that he can speak well. And look, he is also coming out to meet you. When he sees you, he will be glad in his heart. **Exodus 4: 10-14**

Low self-esteem refers to a negative perception of oneself and one's worth, often accompanied by feelings of inadequacy, self-doubt, and a lack of confidence. It can manifest in various ways, including negative self-talk, self-criticism, social withdrawal, and difficulty asserting oneself. People with low self-esteem may struggle with relationships, work, and achieving their goals, as they often feel unworthy or incapable of success. It can also lead to mental health issues such as anxiety and depression.

Moses had considerable doubts about his ability to fulfill his mission because of lack of self-confidence due to his stutter. This strikes a chord with me on a personal level, as I am also someone who stutters. I have faced hurtful mockery due to my struggle with certain syllables when speaking or praying in front of others. Let me tell you about stuttering.

Stuttering is simply horrible. You can have a perfectly intelligent thought process, but it is conveyed as if you were a complete idiot. Nobody would take you seriously. Despite perceiving a sense of dread and embarrassment on people's faces when you are about to speak, you still feel compelled to express your thoughts and embark on that journey of sharing your mind, even though you may not know at what moment you will stop abruptly, never to continue again. You get stuck at the least important part of your sentence (often a word starting with a B, P or M) and everyone gets amused or embarrassed, disregarding then the impact you could have had on the world.

My mind takes me to a church service, at 16 years-old when an elder tapped me on the shoulder and whispered in my ear that I would be doing the offertory prayer. Fear overwhelmed me, causing my inner being to liquefy, and I found myself contemplating strategies to avoid a lifetime of embarrassment in the presence of these good-looking church people. I decided to opt for a short prayer centered around words I could pronounce written on a piece of paper. Despite my efforts, I still stumbled over the words I had carefully chosen. The prayer abruptly ended with a resounding "AMEN" from an exasperated church member, who thought ending the prayer before it ended me was the best course of action for the remainder of the church service. This effectively marked the conclusion of my struggle with a word I thought would be friendly. It always felt like a technical knockout, with the words I struggled with ultimately emerging victorious.

Praying at home during family worship was no different. My parents used to convince me that it was a demon that would take hold of me during prayer and caused me to stutter aggressively. Here I was wondering why the demon would single me out. I had gone through a few deliverance prayers that obviously did not work when I had absolutely no demon at all. This experience has deeply impacted my perception of God, once seen as vast but vastly distant. I began questioning His effectiveness and strength, wondering why He couldn't help me prevent myself from appearing weak and stupid.

The thought of asserting myself both in public and in private was not only discouraging but was terrifying as well. I constantly wondered what would happen if I continued to let others trample over me. What repercussions might arise from suppressing anger, opting for silence, and bottling up emotions due to the fear of being ridiculed? It's worth noting that bottling up emotions and being unable to express them can indeed lead to heightened feelings of frustration, which may find an outlet in violence or other negative behaviors. This has totally been the case for me. There is a specific incident where Moses witnessed an Egyptian beating a Hebrew slave, and in response, he struck and killed the Egyptian, hiding his body in the sand (**Exodus 2:11-12**). While I have never taken someone's life, I have found myself in numerous situations where better emotional management could have led to different outcomes.

For someone like Moses, it could be unconceivable to present himself before such a powerful monarch such as Pharaoh and cock-a-doodle-do his way out of a sentence or luckily two! What about his ego? Instead of embarrassing himself in Egypt, he could have been calmly attending to his father-in-law's flocks in Midian. He adamantly refused to sign up for it and insisted that not even God should do it on his behalf. How frequently do we unintentionally prevent ourselves from being instruments of God due to our own insecurities and fears?

However, to this concern, God patiently reminded Moses and myself that He may have breathed the galaxies into existence, but He also knows a thing or two about making him and I speak fluently as well. He patiently and constantly reminds us that our doubts, worries, and fears should not be a concern because His power exceeds them so much so that they do not even factor into His plans. This is not to imply that God is indifferent to the things that make us feel insignificant and small. He does care about them. However, His primary concern lies in the greater possibilities and achievements that can be realized when we surrender ourselves to Him, even if we are unable to see them.

The less self-confidence one has, the more esteem and value God places on them. We can read all throughout the scriptures that God always called the low life, the small, the messy and the unconsidered. The last-born of his father, David was chosen to lead Israel, Gideon from the tribe of Benjamin was chosen to lead Israel to victory with just 300 men. Despite Ruth being a childless widow and a foreigner, God selected her to be one of Jesus' ancestors. God chose to include Rahab, a former prostitute and a clever liar, in a significant role in the Bible. Despite him coming from a highly dysfunctional family, Joseph was chosen by God to save his people from famine, even though his own brothers had sold him into slavery. None of these people made any claim of superiority, to the contrary. Our weakness is in essence God's power. During moments when I viewed God as ineffective, I came to understand that He was equipping me to be effective for His purposes. It became clear to me that in God's greater plan, our qualifications are found within our very lack of qualifications. We cannot do anything to disqualify ourselves as candidates for God's work and there's no limit to what God can do with broken people. He believes in us. Let me scratch that. He believes He can do anything with us.

What would make His anger kindle against us, however, is when we reject the specific calling, He placed on our lives for the sake of someone else! When we prioritize our ego over the miraculous works that God wants to accomplish in our lives, it must be frustrating for a patient God who is known to be slow to anger. God may be all powerful, omniscient, and all-wise but our uniqueness makes us useful in His specific masterplan. We are in no way disposable! Moses was the one God chose for that moment and Him alone just like we are today in our various capacities.

Let's not disappoint Him!

You are Enough

This is poem from fragile heart, where doubts reside,
Here thrives the haunting whispers of wounded pride.
A fragile soul adorned with shadows of doubt,
Low self-esteem, a relentless foe throughout.

As a silent storm insidiously destroys the beams
it clouds the mind's eye,
Casting shadows over worth, questioning why.
A relentless critic, it tears at the seams,
Leaving scars hidden, though eroding self-esteem.

The mirror reflects a distorted reflection,
Magnifying flaws, igniting self-rejection.
Self-destruction
Insecurities breed, taking root deep within,
Convincing the heart that it can never win.

But beneath the weight of doubt, a light still glows,
A spark of resilience that steadily grows.
For in the midst of darkness, hope can be found,
Embracing self-acceptance, standing on solid ground.

Embrace the uniqueness that makes you whole,
For flaws and imperfections shape your soul.
You are a masterpiece, a work of art divine,
A tapestry woven with threads that intertwine.

Rise above the whispers of self-doubt's refrain,
For you are worthy, despite the internal pain.
Embrace the journey of self-discovery,
Unveil His strength that lies within, so free.

Surround yourself with love, both gentle and kind,
And let self-compassion heal the wounded mind.
Remember, in this vast world, you have a place,
A unique presence that no one can replace.

In the tapestry of life, you play a vital role,
Embrace your worth, and let your spirit unfold.
For low self-esteem may linger, but it cannot preside,
The beautiful essence that resides deep inside.
Yours Truly

For you see your calling, brethren, that not many wise according to the flesh, not many mighty, not many noble, are called. But God has chosen the foolish things of the world to put to shame the wise, and God has chosen the weak things of the world to put to shame the things which are mighty; and the base things of the world and the things which are despised God has chosen, and the things which are not, to bring to nothing the things that are, that no flesh should glory in His presence. But of Him you are in Christ Jesus, who became for us wisdom from God—and righteousness and sanctification and redemption— **1 Corinthians 1:26-30**

11. Why is it so Hard?

So, Moses returned to the Lord and said, "Lord, why have You brought trouble on these people? Why is it You have sent me? For since I came to Pharaoh to speak in Your name, he has done evil to this people; neither have You delivered Your people at all." **Exodus 5: 22-23**

When was the last time you felt obeying God seemed to have led to more problems than solutions? I have a friend who, right after being baptized, was forced to leave his parents' house, and ended up homeless on the streets! The children of Israel, who were already overworked in their enslaved state, had to face the added difficulty of finding their own straw for making the same number of bricks when Moses angered Pharaoh by conveying God's message. They questioned his purpose for showing up and adding to their already miserable existence. During times of comparable difficulty, it is common for us, like Moses, to question the significance of obeying God and to wonder why He appears to willingly permit us to endure such hardships.

The answer lies in His divine design, which can be seen in our bodies through the process of metabolism. Metabolism is the mysterious interplay between destruction and construction that sustains our lives. Metabolism refers to the chemical processes that occur within a living organism to maintain life. These processes include *catabolism*, the breakdown of molecules to obtain energy, and *anabolism,* the synthesis of molecules needed for growth and maintenance. Metabolism involves a complex network of biochemical reactions that convert food into energy and building blocks for the body, as well as the elimination of waste products.

Catabolism is a process that dismantles you from within. It dismantles the image of a self-sufficient and confident person, breaking it into fragments without providing a clear path for reconstruction. It destroys the version of yourself that you believed was perfected and had everything figured out, forcing you back to square one. It entails saying goodbye to loved ones and letting go of attachments forever, leaving you feeling alone, empty, and devoid of hope. Catabolism is undoubtedly a challenging and arduous experience.

As Christians we largely prefer the process of anabolism referring to the buildup and amassing of blessings, the filling up of the barns. We forget that to have the factors required for the buildup, a breakdown was previously necessary. We often tend to talk about God's blessings when everything is going well, but we neglect to acknowledge them during challenging times. However, the truth is that we are blessed simply because God chose us to be part of His plan during a specific period in the history of the universe. He has shown favor towards us and has entrusted us with a significant role to play, just like a coach who strategically sends in a player during the last minutes of a losing game because they believe that player can turn the game on its head. God has chosen us for a purpose, believing in our potential to make a positive impact in a dying world.

Walking with God in obedience often entails facing catabolic circumstances that are intended to shape and prepare us for the subsequent anabolic phase. These challenging situations, though difficult to endure and difficult to make sense of, serve a purpose in our spiritual growth and transformation. They break down our self-reliance, pride, and preconceived notions, allowing God to rebuild us according to His divine plan. While catabolic experiences may initially be disheartening, they ultimately pave the way for the anabolic work of restoration, renewal, and greater alignment with God's purposes. Through obedience and trust, we can embrace these circumstances as opportunities for growth and allow God to bring forth new life and abundant blessings in our journey with Him.

As both phases are part of His plan, we ought to rejoice that we are still part of it! Even amid feeling broken down and scattered, like the individual nucleotides that form a well-functioning and complex nucleic acid, there is hope for restoration. Though it may seem humanly impossible to rebuild what has been dismantled, God has the power to bring healing and wholeness to our lives. Just as the scattered amino acids can be reassembled into a complex and purposeful quaternary protein structure, God can gather the broken pieces of our lives and rebuild us in a way that surpasses our previous state. Through His grace and transformative power, we can experience restoration, renewal, and a greater sense of purpose. While the process may be challenging and require patience, we can trust that God's ultimate plan is to bring us to a place of beauty and strength.

There's not a better example than Job's. He lost it all except his wife and his health. The only thing he did wrong was to come up in a conversation between God and the devil. He walked uprightly in all his ways and there was not a man like him on earth- **Job 1:8**. Yet He was still handed the catabolic treatment. So instead of wondering why "bad things" happen to "good people", we should really ask why not? Despite the inclination to curl up and weep during the catabolic phase, let us rejoice in anticipation of what lies ahead! Jesus Himself said *"Destroy this temple, and in three days I will raise it up"* in **John 2:19**, because there is no doubt over the normal process and His reconstruction will comes after destruction. Even God can break me, but He will but me back together. Life will come after death eventually. After every night, there is a new day; after tears, there is laughter; and after sorrow, there is joy to be found. This is metabolism for you.

The Good news is, the Lord NEVER allows a breakdown without a restorative buildup! Even if the breakdown results in the loss of our own lives, it will still contribute to buildup of something else in God's master plan, because we are only tiny pieces of a grander puzzle. We should humbly remember that we entered this world without any control, and if we surrender our will to His, God will faithfully guide us through our existence. Despite the pain we may experience, which God understands, we must keep trusting in His divine wisdom and acknowledge that He has complete control over our lives, just as He always has.

The lot is cast into the lap,
But its every decision is from the Lord. -- **Proverbs 16:33**

12. The Last-minute Rescue God

And Moses said to the people, "Do not be afraid. Stand still, and see the salvation of the Lord, which He will accomplish for you today. For the Egyptians whom you see today, you shall see again no more forever. The Lord will fight for you, and you shall hold your peace."
Exodus 14: 13-14

I had longed to pursue my studies at Oakwood University located in Huntsville, AL for a considerable time. Being in my home country of Cameroon, I often visited cyber cafes where I would spend hours of my free time browsing the Oakwood University website and listening to WJOU, formerly known as WOCG, online. With fervent prayers, I beseeched the Lord to help me achieve my dream, which was to study there and remarkably, He did! The memory of my first day on the Oakwood University campus remains etched in my mind. I felt acknowledged, cared for, and cherished by a God I thought I had known.

Until the day came when I wondered if He was even there at all. I started *Spring 2010* semester with a balance of $14,562. 65. Clearing 70% of the fees required for registration seemed nearly impossible for me financially. Even with the considerable help my uncle provided, it was not enough to cover the bill. My mother who had just buried my brother had to take on debt back home just to send $1300, which ended up being insufficient and vanished like a coin in murky waters in the vastness of that balance. The poor lady had to continue paying that debt for the next 2 years. I was able to attend the classes I had registered for the previous semester, thanks to my teachers' help and support, even though it was not technically allowed.

Every day was a struggle to get by. On a Greyhound bus bound for campus, my luggage vanished, along with crucial documents. All I possessed were the garments on my back, faithfully worn from weeks of diligent washing, until a kind friend bestowed upon me a fresh wardrobe. Amid the harsh Alabama winter, I found myself wandering on campus, desperately seeking shelter for the night. As I roamed, a glimmer of hope appeared when I stumbled upon an empty suite adorned with cozy couches in Edwards Hall. A smile graced my face as I entered, grateful for the temporary respite from the polar temperatures it offered. However, my slumber was abruptly interrupted by a well-intentioned residential assistant, faithfully carrying out his duties, who kindly requested that I vacate the suite. Reluctantly, I complied and resumed my search for refuge. Eventually, I found solace under a nearby tree, enduring freezing temperatures that chilled not only the body but also the very essence of my thoughts. Miraculously, I found myself relying solely on my pathetically thin coat as a feeble shield against the bitter cold, guarding me from the imminent threat of hypothermia.

Fortunately, I was given the opportunity to sleep on the floor of a classmate's room for the subsequent nights since I wasn't allowed room and board. Whenever a residential assistant came for "room check", I had to act dignified as if I was just visiting my host. For food, I had to station myself by the cafeteria door every day, hoping that someone would kindly swipe their card for me. I often noticed the familiar looks of disgust and contempt on the faces of my fellow students as they routinely saw me there. I had never felt more abandoned by God in my life. I had absolutely nothing.

Negative and bitter thoughts overwhelmed me as I contemplated, " All I desired was an education, now hanging in the balance, why does God allow my classmates to flaunt their wealth and fancy cars before me?" I found it disheartening that some of my classmates, whose tuition had been paid, did not even bother attending classes. Meanwhile, I diligently showed up every day, yet I faced the challenge of not having a place to stay and food security. It seemed unjust that, despite my unwavering dedication, I was deprived of the equal opportunities and support that my peers received, coming from a God whom I believed loved me. I struggled to comprehend His sense of justice, as it often appeared perplexing to me during those days. These were moments when His actions seemed so unjust that I was led to question whether He was just intentionally cruel and seeking my imminent destruction. I had stopped praying. I reached a point in my faith where I began to perceive that God would act according to His own will, and my own desires no longer held significance. I doubted that He would listen to me, as it seemed that He was preoccupied with ministering to others and attending to their needs. Uncertainty loomed over me as I grappled with the fear of losing the semester. The prospect of continuing to sleep on the floor, sandwiched between two dorm room beds like an insignificant creature, filled me with unease. Unfortunately, I had no answers to these pressing questions that weighed heavily on my mind.

Maintaining my student status in the United States as an international student depended on my ability to pay my balance through registration. Failing to do so put my stay in the country at risk. I was informed by the Office of Financial Affairs that my inability to register for that semester would result in me being reported to the Department of Homeland Security, with the possibility of being deported. Begging and pleading did nothing to change the mind of my interlocutor. This was, I thought, the nail on my coffin. Would I have come to Oakwood University just to taste the experience and drop out miserably? It was too difficult for my 21-year-old mind to come to terms with. I wholeheartedly identified myself as an academic being, finding immense joy in the world of education. School was not just a routine for me; it was my passion. I thrived in the classroom, cherishing the knowledge imparted by professors and the challenges presented by tests and assignments. My identity was intricately tied to the subjects I studied and the books I devoured. Given these circumstances, the thought of dropping out and being sent back home was inconceivable. It was something I simply could not fathom, as it went against the core of who I believed myself to be. What about my dream of getting a doctoral degree? My head was spinning at great speed.

I then resolved to put an end to my excruciating anxiety. On that day April 19th, 2010, as the semester was wrapping up, I decided to end my life. I thought nothing would save me from this ordeal. Like the Israelites facing the Red Sea with the sight of a powerful army chasing after them, I felt as though I was doomed. I knew I was doomed. God all the sudden, seemed as silent as a whisper in a secret's keep. It thus seemed probable that God would remain silent as I quietly retreated to where I originated from, without any divine intervention or interference from Him. I went by a well-known site on Campus called the "*Unity Pond*" to drink a previously prepared bottle filled with a solution of sodium hypochlorite pilfered from the dorm's cleaning room that was left open the night before. As I made my walk to that site, I knew I was not going to retrace my steps ever again. With firm resolve, I embarked on a resolute walk towards the culmination of my distress, determined to bring an end to my suffering. While the thought of my lifeless body being discovered by someone was unsettling, I felt compelled to leave it under the open sky, as if to hold solely God accountable for the events that unfolded. I sat down by an oak tree and resigned myself to my fate. I regretfully remembered my mother and how much she would be destroyed by that decision, but it did nothing to stop me.

As I took a sip, I distinctly heard a voice telling me to go back to my classmate's room. It felt like a surreal moment, one, I thought, that usually happens in near-death experiences. However, doubts crept in, and I wondered if I was starting to experience auditory hallucinations. Perhaps this was the final evidence that I had to finish the deadly drink and embrace my demise for good, because nobody likes a broke friend who "hears things".

It happened three times. It was a voice as gentle as the rustling of leaves in the beginning of spring. It carried no trace of reproach, disregarding the very fact that I was about to shut off my hearing forever. I then stood up. Spit out the toxic liquid which had started to bitterly corrode my mucous membranes and made my way to the room. As soon as I arrived, I was informed someone had called specifically for me on the room phone and that they would call back since I was away.

I sat there reminiscing about what had just taken place and wondered how in the world I was still here. A lady Julie V. returned the call, an unfamiliar voice to my ears. We had not conversed prior, yet she seemed acquainted with my name through unknown channels. She took my problem as her own and never gave up until I was cleared. I gained a mother in that moment, until this very day.

The following day, I attended my Genetics class, and, towards the end of the session, my professor summoned me. She requested that I stay back as she wanted to take me somewhere. Surprisingly, I joined her in her car, and we headed to a bank. She asked me to wait patiently while she returned with an envelope containing $2000 admonishing me to put it towards my balance. Overwhelmed with emotion, tears welled up in my eyes as I came to the profound realization of how mistaken I had been about God.

Everything was paid so much that an excess of $85.65 was posted on my balance as credit on that semester. I remain perplexed by the unexplained deposit of $6500.00 that appeared in my account balance during the *Spring 2011* semester, on the following year. Its origin remains a mystery to me to this day. There is absolutely no doubt that God was completely and wholeheartedly involved in these miraculous events. I have unwavering certainty that God was attentively observing every detail as the situation unfolded, right up until the precise moment I contemplated giving up. At times, in our quest to comprehend God's love and His ways, He may allow us to entertain negative thoughts or misconceptions about Him from the difficulties we experience. However, with great delight, He stands ready to prove us wrong and reveal the truth of His character and boundless love, at the last minute.

Our faith is anchored in a God who specializes in last-minute rescues. He's the dawn of deliverance, He's the wealth of all wisdom, His love is limitless, His Word is wonderful, His Reign is righter, His yoke is easy and His burden is light. Oh, I wish I could introduce you to Him adequately, but He's indescribably irresistible. He's simply invincible, He's incomprehensible. He's incomparable. You can live with Him but you can't live without Him. Yes, the Pharisees, they tested Him, but they found out they couldn't defeat Him. Pilate couldn't find any fault in Him, Herod couldn't harm Him, Death couldn't handle Him and the grave couldn't hold Him. That's my God, that's my Christ, that's my Lord, that's my Jesus. Thine is kingdom, the power and glory, Forever and Ever!

He takes delight in demonstrating that it was His intervention, leaving no room for chance or coincidence. These acts are orchestrated so that we can confidently declare that it was Him! For the Israelites, it was the miraculous closing of the Red Sea just as Pharaoh's mighty army was closing in on them. For me, it was the unexpected provision of funds to pay off my school balance before jeopardizing my semester and my life. And for you, it may be the imminent breakthrough you are anticipating. It is the same faithful God, and His ways remain unchanged. Therefore, place your trust in the process, better yet, in the God of the process, knowing that He is tirelessly fighting your battles behind the scenes!

This experience had inspired me to write this poem entitled:

A Silent God

A God as silent as the moon on a cloudless night,

Is a stillness embracing the world, calm and quiet.

No prayers answered yet, no sound to be heard,

It is a serene hush, like the flight of a bird.

A God as silent as a whisper in a secret's keep,

Is His secret plans being shared in the silence deep.

Take time to bask in the gentle breeze rustling the leaves with care,

But the silence remains, floating in the air.

A God as silent as a snowflake, descending from above,

Is softly landing, covering the earth with love.

No sound can capture its beauty and grace,

Only the silent embrace of a trustful heart delicate trace.

A God as silent as a starry sky, vast and serene,

Millions of lights, a cosmic scene.

No shout can describe the wonders above,

Only the silent tireless prayer, the reverence thereof.

A God as silent as a heart, holding its desires,

Can yearn unspoken pain, fueling inner fires.

But a silent longing, hides deep within,

Waiting to be heard, but afraid to begin.

A God as silent as the night, a tapestry of dreams,
In the silence, hope flickers and gleams.
No words are needed to convey its might,
For in the silence, faith takes flight.

A God as silent as a moment of introspection and peace,
Where inner voices whisper, worries cease.
In the quiet depths of the soul's retreat,
Silence teaches patience, in whispers sweet.

A God as silent as the depths of a timeless sea,
Mysteries unfolding, as far as the eye can see.
No tears can fathom its depths so vast,
Only the silent expectation, meant to last.

A God as silent as a vow, sealed with love and trust,
Is the quiet exchange, where hearts intertwine and adjust.
No one can capture the depth of devotion,
Only the silent promise from the scriptures, the faithful solution.

A God as silent as the universe, expanding without end,
Grows in the silence, where cosmic symphonies blend.
No words can contain its infinite expanse,
Only the silent praise, as we gaze in a trance.

A God as silent as the moments that take our breath away,
In the absence of words, emotions can find their way.
For sometimes, in the silence, we truly understand,
That silent trust can speak louder than words ever can.
Yours truly

It is better to take refuge in the Lord than to trust in man. -- **Psalm 118:8**

13. The Beauty of Holiness

Who is like You, O Lord, among the gods?

Who is like You, glorious in holiness,

Fearful in praises, doing wonders? **Exodus 15:11**

When we say that God is holy, we are referring to His absolute moral purity and perfection. God's holiness sets Him apart from all creation and emphasizes His perfect righteousness and goodness. It signifies that He is separate from sin and evil. God's holiness also highlights the vast difference between His nature and our fallen human nature. His holiness demands reverence, awe, and worship. It is a central aspect of His character and serves as a standard for us to strive for in our relationship with Him. God's holiness is a reminder of His transcendence, His perfect moral nature, and the need for us to approach Him with humility and reverence.

The holiness of God permeates the entire narrative of Scripture, serving as its foundation. God's holiness establishes an unchanging moral order where good and evil are not subjective but grounded in God's standards. Human flourishing is intricately linked to aligning with God's desires and finding joy in what pleases Him.

God's absolute moral purity, or holiness, indeed carries a sense of awe. In the context of Israel, there was a fear of getting too close to God, as His holiness was seen as both comforting and threatening. His presence brought comfort to those who sought His guidance and protection, but it also posed a danger to their own sinful lives. Approaching God required a deep sense of seriousness and sincerity. It was not a casual or superficial act. Often, a mediator was needed to intercede on behalf of individuals, as being in the presence of

God's absolute holiness without personal holiness could have severe consequences. The concept of holiness in relation to God emphasizes the need for purity and the recognition of the vast difference between His nature and our fallen state.

God's ultimate desire, spanning from the beginning of Genesis to the end of Revelation, is to transform the entire universe into a sacred abode for Himself. This longing finds its fulfillment in the future culmination of His plan, depicted in the new heavens and new earth as described in **Revelation 21-22**. This grand vision harks back to the original state of the garden of Eden portrayed in **Genesis 2-3**, where God established a place of abundant goodness. However, the ultimate fulfillment of this plan goes beyond the restoration of what was lost in the garden. Through the redemptive work of Jesus, it encompasses the complete formation of a people who belong to God and are fully embraced within His presence and holiness, finding their true home in Him.

A call To Holiness

From Egypt's chains, a nation set free,
To walk with God, in His presence to be.
He declares, "I am the Lord, your guide,
Be holy, for I am holy," He does confide.

In His mighty hand, He led them forth,
Through desert sands, toward a new birth.
A covenant formed, a people chosen,
To showcase His holiness, His glory unbroken.

The voice of the Almighty, powerful and true,
Resounds through ages, reaching me and you.
"I am your God," His words resound,
A call to holiness, with purpose profound.

For He, the Holy One, pure and divine,
Calls us to a life of righteousness, a sacred design.
To walk in His ways, His truth to embrace,
Reflecting His holiness, adorned with grace.

From slavery to freedom, a profound story,
He rescued His people, revealed His glory.
And now, as His chosen, we're called to display,
The holiness of our God, in all our own ways.

In our thoughts and actions, in words we speak,
In compassion and love, to the hurting we seek.
For holiness beckons us, a higher call,
To reflect our God, to stand tall.

With hearts surrendered, our lives transformed,
We seek His presence, our spirits warmed.
Through His Spirit, He empowers our soul,
To be holy as He is, our ultimate goal.

So let us arise, in reverence and fear,
Embracing His holiness, drawing near.
For He is the Lord, our God divine,
We shall be holy, for His glory to shine.
Yours Truly

For I am the Lord who brought you up out of the land of Egypt to be your God. You shall therefore be holy, for I am holy. --- **Leviticus 11:45**

14. Trust the Process

Then the Lord said to Moses, "Behold, I will rain bread from heaven for you. And the people shall go out and gather a certain quota every day, that I may test them, whether they will walk in My law or not..." **Exodus 16: 4**

In **Exodus 3:8** God promises to take the children of Israel out of slavery to a good and large land where *"milk and honey"* flows in abundance. This is the plan He has for us as **Jeremiah 29:11** states. However, *"on the fifteenth day of the second month after they departed from the land of Egypt"* on the way to that good and wonderful land, the people in the wilderness, complained of hunger! *"Yes, I know you have plans to prosper me and not to harm me, but I need a job right now, Lord."* How often does our present circumstance drastically fail to match up with what God has promised?

All throughout Exodus 16 there is a recurring pattern among those who indulge in complaint. The people adamantly asserted that Moses and Aaron harbored ill or malicious intentions. Naturally, Moses and Aaron had no desire to harm the people of Israel, making such an accusation utterly unjust. Nevertheless, a heart prone to complaint frequently finds it effortless to impute the worst motives to the person they complain about.

In this world, there is no deeper degradation for human nature than when the body is enslaved by political oppression and the soul is corrupted by the power of sin. The Hebrews in their plight were not only bound as slaves but also burdened by the weight of their transgressions, which rendered them susceptible to the lowest and most dishonorable deeds.

Despite having witnessed the plagues, celebrated Passover, and experienced the miraculous deliverance at the Red Sea, one might assume that Israel would fully acknowledge that it was the LORD who had liberated them from Egypt. However, it is important to recognize that experiences, no matter how profound, and revitalizing do not always have the transformative power we expect them to have on the human heart. To constantly depend on God to prove Himself for us to believe in Him will eventually be as futile as trying to draw blood from a stone.

Nevertheless, God demonstrated His glory by revealing His mercy and goodness. Instead of raining down punishment from heaven, He provided them with bread. He didn't require them to cease their complaints before offering sustenance. Just as Jesus would later instruct us, God extended love and nourishment to those who behaved as His adversaries.

In the wilderness, with only God as their provider, the children of Israel longed for the good meals they used to have as slaves. To what extent must someone feel homesick in order to yearn for a place where suffering was a common occurrence, simply because of the availability of meat? The God of *Milk and Honey* is the same as the God of *Raining Manna.* We're the only ones that tend to change based on the circumstance. We are unable to truly honor Him in times of abundance if we complain when He chooses instead to provide for us Himself day by day. If we fail to learn this lesson, we might find ourselves wandering in the wilderness for "40 years" unable to have access to the place He intended to take us to all along.

Let us rejoice in the journey of being guided by the Lord, whether it's day by day, paycheck to paycheck, or even hour by hour in a hospital bed. It is when we have truly grasped that He doesn't require proof of His trustworthiness that we have successfully overcome the test.

Blessed is the man who trusts in the Lord,

And whose hope is the Lord.

For he shall be like a tree planted by the waters,

Which spreads out its roots by the river,

And will not fear when heat comes.

But its leaf will be green,

And will not be anxious in the year of drought,

Nor will cease from yielding fruit. --- **Jeremiah 17:7-8**

15. Worship Me

And Moses went up to God, and the Lord called to him from the mountain, saying, "Thus you shall say to the house of Jacob, and tell the children of Israel: 'You have seen what I did to the Egyptians, and how I bore you on eagles' wings and brought you to Myself. Now therefore, if you will indeed obey My voice and keep My covenant, then you shall be a special treasure to Me above all people; for all the earth is Mine. And you shall be to Me a kingdom of priests and a holy nation.' These are the words which you shall speak to the children of Israel." **Exodus 19: 3-6**

True worship is grounded in a deep spiritual connection and an authentic understanding of the immeasurable value of God. It goes beyond mere religious rituals or emotional experiences. Genuine worship is rooted in a profound comprehension of God's character and a sincere recognition of His infinite worthiness. It stems from a heart that grasps the depth of God's love, holiness, and sovereignty. It is a response that springs from a correct understanding of who God is and a genuine appreciation of His supreme worth. In true worship, we wholeheartedly acknowledge and honor God's divine attributes, giving Him the reverence and adoration, He deserves.

Indeed, the term "worship" in English originates from the concept of "worth ship." In other words, worship is the act of demonstrating and proclaiming the immeasurable worth of God. It involves showcasing and expressing the inherent value, glory, and significance of God through various means. Worship is not merely a passive acknowledgment but an active demonstration of God's supreme worthiness. It is an intentional display of reverence, adoration, and honor, magnifying the matchless attributes and qualities of the Divine. Through worship, we publicly declare and manifest the worth of God, acknowledging His greatness and exalting Him above all else.

God demanded worship from the children of Israel. The striking aspect of that request is that there was the possibility of an exchange, a deal. If they obeyed His voice and kept His covenant, in return they would be a special treasure to Him above all people because all the earth is His. They shall be a kingdom of priests and a holy nation as the Lord declared. The devil used a similar approach deceitfully when he tried to woo Jesus-Christ in the desert into worshipping him as well. *"To you I will give all this authority and their glory, for it has been delivered to me, and I give it to whom I will. If you, then, will worship me, it will all be yours.* **Luke 4:6-7**.

The devil understands worship invariably results in imparting power. There was no better person to understand it more than Jesus Himself. At his weakest moment, He knew He needed to give allegiance to someone for strength. To the adversary, who accuses and undermines believers, the power that is derived from worshipping him will only be limited to materialistic gains. The concept of "authority" indeed stems from the word "author," and when we reflect upon it, we realize that God is the ultimate Author of the entire universe, as depicted in Genesis 1. Every aspect of creation, including Satan himself, was brought into existence by God's divine hand. It is crucial to remember that Satan, despite his angelic nature, is not divine and is not on equal footing with God.

Satan's role is distorted, as he takes what God has established and twists it into sin. He is the author of lies, manipulating and distorting God's truth for his own malevolent purposes.

If Jesus had yielded and bowed before Satan, it raises an intriguing question: Could Satan truly have delivered "all the kingdoms of the world and their glory" to Jesus, as mentioned in Matthew 4:8? To grasp the essence of this situation, we must consider that kingdoms of the world are composed of people and systems that stand in rebellion against God.

In essence, Satan was attempting to entice Jesus to join his rebellion against God. How would Jesus accomplish this? By choosing to deviate from God's divine plan, which involved humbling himself, devoting His worship to Him and willingly undergoing the pain and suffering of the cross, being raised to new life, and receiving the kingdom of God from his Father (as described in Ephesians 2:5-10). Instead of submitting to God's will and obeying Him, Jesus could have submitted to Satan, bypassing the agonizing journey to the cross, and instantly become the ruler of Satan's renegade kingdom.

However, this alternative path would have been a betrayal of God's purpose and a rejection of His redemptive plan for humanity. Jesus' mission was not to seize earthly power through compromise with evil, but rather to embody sacrificial love and offer salvation to all who believe in Him. By remaining faithful to God's plan, Jesus demonstrated his unwavering devotion and commitment to the kingdom of God, which transcends the temporary and flawed kingdoms of this world.

In this profound moment of temptation, Jesus resolutely chose the way of obedience, worship of the One True God and redemption, paving the way for humanity to be reconciled with God. His ultimate victory over sin and death through the cross and resurrection embodies the triumph of God's divine plan over the deceptive allure of earthly power.

When we worship the God of the Universe by keeping his covenant, He made with us through the blood of Jesus-Christ shed on the cross of calvary, we will be given a form of power well superior to material gains; the type of power all *the princes* and *principalities* shudder at the thought of. The power we obtain from worshipping God places us far above the vicissitudes of anxious life and the concerns of material needs, because as He said, "*All the earth is mine*".

Hence, the adversary tirelessly orchestrates alluring distractions to divert our focus and commitment from God. Our lack of security and frequent stumbling in our Christian journey can be attributed to our self-centered worship. We succumb to the desires of self-indulgence and self-exaltation, which hinder our wholehearted devotion to Christ. We are oblivious to the incredible power that lies within being acknowledged as a "special treasure" to the God of Israel.

"But you are a chosen generation, a royal priesthood, a holy nation, His own special people, that you may proclaim the praises of Him who called you out of darkness into His marvelous light; "---**1 Peter 2:9**

Get thee Behind Me

In the desert's barren expanse, a battle took place,
Where earthly power sought to claim its space.
Jesus, the Son of God, stood firm and strong,
To face the tempter's deceitful throng.

With hunger gnawing deep within His frame,
Satan came forth, eager to defame.
He whispered slyly, "Turn these stones to bread,
Satisfy your hunger, fill your own digestive bed."

But Jesus, resolute, spoke words of might,
"Man shall not live by bread alone," His light.
For He knew the power of God's holy word,
And trusted in the Father, undeterred.

Next, to a lofty pinnacle they ascended,
Satan's voice enticed; pride intended.
"Throw yourself down, the angels will save,
Prove your divinity, and your glory engrave."

Yet Jesus, steadfast, rebuked the deceit,
For tempting God, He would not greet.
His devotion unwavering, His faith secure,

In God's protection, He was sure.

Lastly, on a mountain, the world displayed,
Satan offered power; kingdoms arrayed.
"All this can be yours," the tempter enticed,
"Worship me, and earthly dominion shall suffice."

But Jesus, firm in His heavenly quest,
Declared, "Get behind me, you shall not wrest.
For it is written, 'Worship the Lord alone,
Serve Him faithfully, on His throne.'"

In the face of temptation, Jesus stood tall,
His resolve unyielding, His purpose enthralled.
He conquered the lure of earthly desire,
And in His triumph, lit Heaven's Empire

Let us learn from Christ's steadfast fight,
To overcome darkness with God's holy light.
In the temptations we face, let us stand,
With faith as our shield, in God's mighty hand.

For in His victory, we find redemption's grace,
A Savior who withstood temptation's embrace.
His example guides us, His strength we implore,
To resist the tempter, forevermore.

Yours Truly

16. A Faithful God

Know therefore that the LORD your God is God; he is the faithful God, keeping his covenant of love to a thousand generations of those who love him and keep his commandments. **Deuteronomy 7:9**

A faithful friend is someone who stands by your side through thick and thin, demonstrating unwavering support and loyalty. This friend is trustworthy and reliable, always there when you need them, and willing to lend a listening ear or a helping hand. They keep your confidence, offer honest advice, and genuinely care about your well-being. A faithful friend shows up consistently, even in challenging times, and remains committed to the friendship, fostering a deep sense of trust and companionship.

Like all aspects of God's character, His attributes are not independent or isolated qualities but interconnected components of His perfect and unified being. Therefore, His faithfulness cannot be comprehended without considering His immutability, the quality of being unchanging. When we encounter the statement that God remains faithful because He cannot deny Himself, we witness the harmony of these attributes at work. The very nature of His unchanging being ensures that He can never act contrary to His faithfulness.

God is completely trustworthy and reliable. His promises are always true and certain. In every interaction and relationship with His people, God demonstrates unwavering faithfulness. Those who place their trust in Him will never be disappointed. Throughout the Scriptures, we repeatedly encounter this profound truth, as it is vital for His people to understand that faithfulness is an integral aspect of God's nature. It is the very foundation of our confidence in Him, knowing that we can rely on Him completely.

God's infinite and unwavering faithfulness signifies that He has a flawless memory, never fails in His actions and commitments, and remains steadfast in His promises without any change of heart. This faithfulness is an overflow of His boundless love, which assures us that we can confidently rely on Paul's affirmation that God, in His providence, *"... works for the good of those who love him."*

Certainly, there are instances when we may struggle to comprehend or perceive God's faithfulness in the midst of our circumstances. From our limited understanding and finite perspectives, it might even appear as if God has forsaken us, leading us to question His faithfulness. However, we must remember that God's ways are higher than our ways, and His thoughts are higher than our thoughts. Despite our limited understanding, we can trust that God's faithfulness remains unwavering, even when we are unable to see it clearly. His faithfulness is not contingent on our understanding, but on His unchanging nature.

If we are faithless,
He remains faithful.
He cannot deny Himself. --- **2 Timothy 2:13**

17. An Eternal God

For I lift up my hand to heaven and swear, As I live forever. **Deuteronomy 32:40**

When we say that God is eternal, we mean that God exists outside of time and is not bound by its limitations. Unlike created beings, who are subject to the passage of time and have a beginning and an end, God transcends time and is unchanging in His existence. Here are a few key aspects of what it means when we describe God as eternal:

Timelessness: God's existence is not confined to any particular point in time. He exists in an eternal present that encompasses all moments past, present, and future. This means that God does not experience a sequence of events or undergo any changes in His being. He is the same yesterday, today, and forever. One way to grasp the timelessness of God is to consider the analogy of an author and a book. Imagine an author writing a story. The author is not subject to the sequential unfolding of events within the story but stands outside of it, overseeing the entire narrative. The author can see the beginning, the middle, and the end all at once. Similarly, God, as the creator and sustainer of time, exists beyond its confines, observing all moments simultaneously. God's timelessness is expressed in various ways. In **Psalm 90:2**, it says, "*Before the mountains were born or you brought forth the whole world, from* *everlasting to everlasting you are God."* This verse highlights that God is eternal, without a beginning or an end. He exists beyond the boundaries of time and is not subject to its limitations. Another biblical passage that speaks to God's timelessness is **2 Peter 3:8**, which says, *"But do not forget this one thing, dear friends: With the Lord, a day is like a thousand years, and a thousand years are like a day."* This verse emphasizes that God's perspective of time is vastly different from ours. What may seem like a long period of time to us is but a fleeting moment to God. The timelessness of God has profound implications for our understanding of His nature and actions. It means that God's knowledge is not limited by time but encompasses all things. He knows the past, present, and future with perfect clarity. It also means that God's promises and purposes are unchanging. His faithfulness extends throughout all of time, and His plans are not subject to alteration or revision. Furthermore, God's timelessness assures us of His constant presence and accessibility. He is not confined by temporal limitations and is always available to hear our prayers and respond to our needs. Whether we perceive His response immediately or in the passage of time, God's timeless nature guarantees that He is ever attentive to His creation.

Uncreated and Uncaused: God is not subject to the limitations of a temporal origin. He has no beginning or end but exists necessarily and independently. The concepts of the uncreatedness and uncausedness of God are fundamental to understanding His nature as the ultimate source of all existence. They affirm that God is not dependent on anything or anyone else for His existence but is self-existent and self-sufficient.

He exists outside the realm of created beings and is not subject to the limitations of time, space, or causality. Unlike everything else in the universe, which is contingent and derived from something else, God exists necessarily and independently. Recognizing His self-existence nature invites us to approach Him reverence. It reminds us that He is the ultimate reality, the ground of all beings, and the source of our existence. It also encourages us to trust in His providence and sovereignty, knowing that He is not subject to the confines and uncertainties of the created world. The idea of God's uncreatedness can be challenging for our finite minds to comprehend fully. Our experience is shaped by the reality of cause and effect, where everything we encounter has a cause that precedes it. However, God transcends this causal chain. He is the First Cause, the uncaused Cause from which all things derive their existence.

Infinite Duration: God's eternity is not limited by duration or duration itself. It is not a mere extension of time but encompasses an infinite and boundless existence. God is not subject to the passage of time or any temporal constraints. The infinite duration of God is closely related to His immutability, or unchanging nature. God does not experience growth, decay, or temporal progression. He is eternally consistent and constant in His being, character, and purposes. This immutability is rooted in His infinite duration, as time itself cannot impact or alter the eternal nature of God. Understanding the infinite duration of God has profound implications for our understanding of His relationship with creation and with humanity. God's eternal existence means that He has always been and will always be present. He is not limited by the boundaries of time and space but is intimately involved in every moment of history.

Omnipresence: God's eternity is intimately connected to His omnipresence. Being outside of time, God is present at all points in time simultaneously. He is not confined by spatial limitations but is present everywhere and in all moments. The concept of God's omnipresence is deeply rooted in Scripture. In **Psalm 139:7-10**, the psalmist declares, "*Where can I go from your Spirit? Where can I flee from your presence? If I go up to the heavens, you are there; if I make my bed in the depths, you are there. If I rise on the wings of the dawn, if I settle on the far side of the sea, even there your hand will guide me, your right hand will hold me fast.*" This passage highlights the all-encompassing nature of God's presence, affirming that He is present in every corner of the universe. The omnipresence of God also has significant implications for our understanding of His relationship with creation. It means that God is intimately aware of every detail and aspect of our lives. He is not distant or detached but actively involved in the world He has created. His presence extends to every moment, circumstance, and situation, offering comfort, guidance, and support to those who seek Him. God's omnipresence is not merely a passive observation of creation but also an active engagement with it. He sustains and upholds the universe through His presence, maintaining order and fulfilling His purposes. His omnipresence is a source of comfort, knowing that we are never alone and that God is always with us, even in the midst of trials and challenges.

Immutable Nature: God's eternality also implies His unchanging nature. He is not subject to the fluctuations or variations that occur within time. God's character, attributes, and purposes remain constant throughout eternity.

Everlasting Life: The eternal nature of God has implications for the life He offers to believers. Through faith in God, individuals can experience a relationship with Him that transcends the temporal and enter into everlasting life. This eternal life is not limited by time or death but is a participation in God's own eternal existence.

It is important to note that the concept of God's eternality goes beyond our human comprehension. Our understanding of time is rooted in our finite existence, and we struggle to fully grasp the infinite and timeless nature of God. The language and concepts we use to describe God's eternality are limited by our human perspective.

Your throne is established from of old; you are from everlasting. --- **Psalm 93:2**

To the One who Lives Forever

In the confines of the Cosmos beyond our mortal sight,
Where time liquefies in endless light,
There dwells a Being, vast and grand,
Whose essence spans eternity's expanse.

Before the birth of time and space,
Before the universe found its place,
I AM stood, unbound by temporal chains,
Eternal, with no beginning or end to claim.

No measure can confine His might,
No boundaries restrict His eternal flight,
For in His essence, timeless and pure,
He reigns, forever and ever more.

From everlasting to everlasting, He remains,
Unfettered by the constraints that bind our days,
A steady beacon, a constant flame,
The Alpha and Omega, the Eternal Name.

No clock can mark His endless reign,
No calendar can measure His domain,
For in His presence, time dissolves
As eternity's weavings forever unfolds.

Though we, in finite mortal guise,
Strive to grasp what lies beyond our eyes,
We find peace in the eternal embrace,
Of a God whose love knows no time or space.

In Him, our weary hearts find rest,
In Him, our souls are truly blessed,
For His eternal nature, steadfast and true,
Offers hope, redemption, and life anew.

I will marvel at the eternal flame,
That burns within His hallowed name,
And with humble hearts and voices raised,
Praise the Eternal God, worthy of our praise.
Yours Truly

18. It's Just a Test

Then the anger of the Lord was hot against Israel; and He said, "Because this nation has transgressed My covenant which I commanded their fathers, and has not heeded My voice, I also will no longer drive out before them any of the nations which Joshua left when he died, so that through them I may test Israel, whether they will keep the ways of the Lord, to walk in them as their fathers kept them, or not." **Judges 2: 20-22**

One of the unmistakable demonstrations of God's character, as revealed in Scripture, is His unwavering engagement on behalf of His beloved children. Throughout the Old Testament, we witness His active involvement in the lives of the Israelites, His chosen people. In the New Testament, we observe His continuous care for the Church. However, it can be perplexing to comprehend how He responds to His children when we find ourselves plunging into the depths of sin.

God, unlike us, does not abandon people when they fail. His love is unwavering and nothing can separate us from it in Christ Jesus. He remains tirelessly committed to His adopted children, always working on their behalf. However, it is important to recognize that some of His actions can be misunderstood.

When we encounter God's judgments upon His own children, we should view them through the lens of His loving discipline aimed at leading us to repentance. The writer of Hebrews reminds us that God disciplines those He loves, much like a caring father who seeks our ultimate good. Though the experience of corrective discipline may initially be accompanied by sorrow, its ultimate outcome is the cultivation of a "*peaceful fruit of righteousness*" (Hebrews 12:11).

So, how does God's discipline manifest? It can take on both active and passive forms. At times, God directly sends judgments as a means of discipline. However, there are other instances when He chooses to withdraw His hand. The writer of Lamentations provides an insightful evaluation of God's discipline upon Israel.

In Lamentations 2:3, the writer describes how God, in His fierce anger, has severed Israel's strength and withdrawn His right hand from before their enemies. The right hand of God symbolizes His power, and it is through His right hand that He often saves and protects His people. In this particular instance, God's discipline upon Israel involved the passive act of removing His protective hand from them.

In Judges 2:20-22, it is disclosed that when God withdraws His saving right hand, it is done with the intention of testing His people to see if they would come back to Him or stay in their ways. God, possessing unlimited power and wisdom, has granted every individual the gift of free will, which He upholds within the boundaries of His laws.

All God can do is evoke a response from us when confronted with the outcomes of our actions. The choice is ours: will we relent and repent, or will we rebel and remain unyielding? God will not coerce or compel us in any way.

The Test

In the crucible of life's trials, we find,
God's testing hand, gentle and kind.

He sees the strength within our soul,
And with loving purpose, He makes us whole.

Like gold refined in the fiery heat,
God's testing molds us, oh so fleet.
Through trials and struggles, we are refined,
For His divine purpose, we are designed.

With wisdom and grace, He carefully crafts,
The challenges we face, the mountains we're tasked.
For amid trials, we often discover,
Our need for Him, as our faithful lover.

In the wilderness, He leads us to roam,
To find our way back, to return to our home.
He tests our hearts, our faith, and our will,
To draw us closer, His love to instill.

Though the road may be rough, and tears may fall,
God's testing is a gentle, loving call.
He wants us to know His unwavering care,
To seek His presence, in fervent prayer.

For in the testing, our spirits grow,
We learn to trust, to let His love show.
Through trials endured, we find our way,
To surrender to Him, day by day.

So let us embrace the tests that come,
Knowing God's purpose will not be undone.
For in His wisdom, He tests and refines,
To shape us into vessels that truly shine.

In the trials, we find strength and grace,
To draw closer to God, seek His face.
For His desire, in love and trust,
Is to test us, refine us, and make us just.
Yours Truly

The Lord tests the righteous,
But the wicked and the one who loves violence His soul hates.
Psalms 11:5

19. A Lover of Praise

And the Lord said to Gideon, "The people who are with you are too many for Me to give the Midianites into their hands, lest Israel claim glory for itself against Me, saying, 'My own hand has saved me. **Judges 7:2**

The act of entering the Lord's presence is accompanied by praise and gratitude, which He greatly honors. The Lord holds a special affection for praise; the exalted and sacred One resides within the praises of His people. The aroma of the Lord is found in the sweet perfume of His children's praises. He delights in the fragrance that emanates from our worship and prayers, much like the captivating scent of blooming flowers.

Everything in existence was designed to bring glory to the Lord, and every created thing was intended to offer praise to Him. Like a vast symphony, God's magnificent creation resounds with living melodies. "All nature sings of Christ our King!" It is as if even the rocks themselves cry out to the Lord, lifting their voices in adoration. Even the humblest and most unattractive creatures can extol the Lord and sing praises to Jesus. Even the lowliest and most scorned creatures can raise their voices in joyful song. The entirety of His creation gives Him praise; they all declare His glory!

At times, we may be tempted to view God's desire for praise as rooted in vanity. However, the irony lies in the fact that when we analyze praise carefully, it rightfully belongs to God, even for the things we mistakenly want to take credit for. This is because God is the ultimate source, as stated in **James 1**, "*He is the source of every good and perfect gift.*" If praise is truly deserved, then it becomes a moral duty. In other words, it is not only fitting for God to receive praise, but we are obligated to offer it to Him. Moreover, we should praise God even for the things we believe deserve our own recognition. By doing so, we acknowledge that claiming credit for His works is a form of theft. It is no surprise, then, that the Psalmist in **Psalm 150:2** writes, "*Praise Him for His mighty deeds, praise Him according to His excellent greatness.*" We express our praise to God for both His actions and His inherent greatness.

Is God a megalomaniac, an excessively self-centered and power-hungry individual? Absolutely not. This question, in its truest sense, is both presumptuous and irresponsible. How could God be anything other than perfect in His nature? Nevertheless, viewed from a different angle, the question can be illuminating, as it directs our thinking to the essence of God's magnificence and resets our theological framework. God manifests His love for us by unveiling His glory and by passionately safeguarding His own name and reputation. Our greatest joy is discovered in beholding His magnificence and in exalting the triune God for all eternity.

As imperfect individuals, our perception is clouded by sin, preventing us from realizing that depriving God of His rightful glory also deprives us of genuine joy. It is solely through God's unmerited favor and kindness that we come to understand this truth. Interestingly, God magnifies His own greatness by unveiling Himself to those trapped in sin and delivering them through Christ's flawless sacrifice for their transgressions.

We have been intricately designed by God in such a way that our very existence serves as a tool for praise. In the book of Revelation, specific passages like **Revelation 4:6–9, 5:6–14, 6:1–8, 14:3, 15:7**, and **19:4** introduce us to a group of beings known as the four living creatures. These passages do not present them as symbolic or metaphorical entities but rather as real and actual beings. These four living creatures, also referred to as cherubim, hold a special and exalted position in the angelic hierarchy, as they are situated near the throne of God. The book of Ezekiel further suggests that they are in constant motion around the divine throne.

What captures my interest is the continuous declaration made by these four beings: "*Holy, holy, holy is the Lord God Almighty, who was and is and is to come!*" I decided to repeat this sacred proclamation multiple times, and to my amazement, it resonated with the rhythm of my own heartbeat. Normal heart sounds are often described as a steady "*lub-dub*" pattern. The initial sound, known as "*lub,*" occurs as the **mitral** and **tricuspid valves** close. Subsequently, the following sound, referred to as **"dub,"** arises when the **aortic** and **pulmonary valves** shut, signifying the completion of the heart's contraction and the expulsion of blood from its chambers. This led me to a realization – could it be mere coincidence that our hearts have four valves responsible for the rhythmic beats we hear? I believe this design was intentional. In the realm of eternal worship, the four living creatures utter their sacred words of praise without ceasing. Similarly, our hearts were meticulously crafted to beat incessantly, embodying a continuous rhythm of life and devotion, had it not been for the intrusion of sin. The intricate design of our hearts and therefore our lives testify to their intended purpose of unwavering praise and adoration.

Let us now delve into **Revelation 4:4**, which states, "*Around the throne were twenty-four thrones, and seated on the thrones were twenty-four elders, clothed in white garments, with golden crowns on their heads.*" At first, this verse may appear insignificant, but when I considered the fact that we have twenty-four ribs perfectly positioned in our chests, mirroring the imagery described in the verse, it took on a deeper meaning. Our very physical composition, with twenty-four ribs resembling thrones, echoes the divine throne of God. With these profound connections, it becomes clear that we are uniquely designed to be instruments of praise. Our very existence, from the rhythm of our hearts to the structure of our chests, reflects the grandeur and majesty of God's throne. How can we not embrace our role as vessels of praise?

God desires to receive the glory, and He alone deserves it. He invites you to offer praise, thanksgiving, and honor to Him because He is the one who accomplishes great things. If it were possible for you to claim credit for His works, you would be tempted to congratulate yourself, boasting about your own greatness and accomplishments. However, speaking in such a manner can lead to trouble. It is crucial to continually acknowledge and proclaim, "Wow, look at what God has done! See the marvelous work of the Lord. Observe His magnificent deeds."

The Angelic Poem

O Heavenly realms, resplendent and bright,
I soar through celestial realms with delight,
As an angelic being, my purpose is clear,
To praise the Almighty, whom I hold dear.

In radiant splendor, with wings unfurled,

I proclaim His glory to all the world,
With voice melodious, like a symphony,
I sing of His love and His majesty.

In His presence, I'm enveloped by light,
Transcending boundaries of earthly sight,
For His grace and mercy, boundless and true,
Illuminate the heavens with hues of blue.

I marvel at His wisdom, vast and profound,
In awe of His creation, all around,
From galaxies scattered across the sky,
To the smallest creatures that flutter by.

The oceans and mountains, majestic and grand,
Display His power, like a master's hand,
The gentle breeze, the morning sunrise,
Reveal His artistry, a wondrous surprise.

Oh, how I adore Him, the Eternal King,
With praises on my lips, I joyfully sing,
His name resounds in angelic harmonies,
Echoing through celestial galaxies.

In ceaseless worship, I bow before His throne,
A seraphic chorus, His glory we intone,
For He is the Alpha, the Omega, the I AM,
The eternal God, the Great "Amen."

So, let us unite, celestial beings above,
In reverence and adoration, pure love,
For in His presence, our spirits take flight,
As we, angelic voices, praise with all our might.

Holy, holy, holy, we proclaim His name,
Throughout eternity, His praises we acclaim,
For in the heavens, forever we shall be,
Angels, devoted in worship, for all to see.
Yours Truly

20. An Unwavering Word

And he cried to the man of God who came from Judah. Thus says the Lord, because you have disobeyed the word of the Lord and have not kept the command the Lord your God commanded you but have come back and have eaten bread and drunk water in the place of which he said to you, 'Eat no bread and drink no water,' your body shall not come to the tomb of your fathers. **1 Kings 13:21–22**

1 Kings 13:21-22 recounts a significant event involving a man of God, a prophet who had spoken boldly on behalf of God. This man had initially obeyed God's word and carried out his instructions faithfully. However, he became deceived and ultimately disobeyed God's command, leading to severe consequences.

The story highlights the danger of partial or temporary obedience to God. Although the man had started well, he allowed himself to be swayed by deception and veered off course. As a result, he faced the ultimate consequence of death. This passage serves as a cautionary tale, reminding us of the importance of wholehearted obedience to God's word. Partial obedience is not sufficient; God expects complete devotion and obedience to His commands. Even a single act of disobedience can have serious repercussions.

The incident also emphasizes the need for discernment and wisdom in our spiritual journey. It emphasizes the significance of following God's commands faithfully and not being swayed by external influences or deceptive words. We must be vigilant against deception and remain steadfast in our commitment to follow God's instructions fully. The consequences of deviating from God's commands can be severe and should not be taken lightly.

Ultimately, this passage prompts us to evaluate our own adherence to God's commands. Are we picking and choosing which parts of His word to obey or merely fulfilling His commands partially? It serves as a reminder of the importance of wholeheartedly surrendering ourselves to God's will and actively seeking His guidance in every area of our lives.

The story in 1 Kings 13:21-22 serves as a powerful reminder of the dangers and consequences of partial obedience and urges us to pursue wholehearted obedience to God's commands, seeking His wisdom and discernment in all our actions and decisions.

He replied, "Blessed rather are those who hear the word of God and obey it." **Luke 11:28**

21. A God in Love with Darkness

While he himself went a day's journey into the desert. He came to a broom tree, sat down under it and prayed that he might die. "I have had enough, LORD," he said. "Take my life; I am no better than my ancestors. "Then he lay down under the tree and fell asleep. All at once an angel touched him and said, "Get up and eat." He looked around, and there by his head was a cake of bread baked over hot coals, and a jar of water. He ate and drank and then lay down again. The angel of the LORD came back a second time and touched him and said, "Get up and eat, for the journey is too much for you." So he got up and ate and drank. Strengthened by that food, he traveled forty days and forty nights until he reached Horeb, the mountain of God. **1 Kings 19: 4-8**

Depression is increasingly prevalent in our modern society, emerging as a significant mental health disorder. It is characterized by persistent feelings of sadness, loss of interest or pleasure in activities. It is more than just feeling sad or going through a temporary rough patch; depression is a prolonged and intense state of emotional distress that can significantly impact a person's daily life, relationships, and overall well-being. Throughout my life, I have grappled with a profound search for meaning and purpose. I have frequently contemplated the enigma of how two individuals of opposite sexes can come together, leading to my own existence, bestowing upon me the responsibility of my own being and life choices, when I never asked to be here in the first place. Frequently, I contemplate the tranquility that exists within the realm of non-existence. I have perpetually faced a struggle to perceive life through the same vibrant lens as others, often pondering why shades of gray hold such allure for everyone else. I often longed to burst into laughter, the kind that sounds funny and quickly becomes contagious, just like the rich and hearty laughter I witnessed from others. Yet, I struggled to find the reasons that would ignite such an experience within me. Such was my battle with depression, a relentless struggle that continues to this day, although not as intense and debilitating as it once was.

Being a prophet is far from an easy task. It entails being a vulnerable and often misunderstood individual, viewed as an outcast and a misfit in society. As a fallible human being, prone to mistakes and imperfections, you carry the weighty responsibility of being a mouthpiece for a powerful and holy God who specifically chose you among others. Despite this honor, you may still find yourself questioning why you were selected for such a significant role. Every day, there is a weighty responsibility to deliver a message as a prophet, even when personal reluctance arises. However, due to the immense greatness God represents, refusing to fulfill this duty is simply not an option. You feel as if your emotions are not considered in the equation. You feel... used, just as you might suggest that we should be by God. Elijah, too, may have likely experienced such sentiments.

With unwavering obedience, Elijah faithfully followed every instruction given to him before witnessing one of the most awe-inspiring miracles orchestrated by God. The divine purpose behind these meticulous actions was to showcase God's unparalleled power to His people, compelling them to abandon their futile devotion to idols that held no true significance. I mean, how do you get fire come down from heaven so hot that it consumes an altar and dries up a trench of about 15 liters of water immediately? He rightfully felt a deep sense of pride in serving the Almighty God, knowing that he stood in allegiance to the most powerful divine Being. As a testament to his unwavering faith, he confronted and defeated the prophets of Baal, eliminating them from the scene and from existence.

However, paradoxically, he experienced a sense of vulnerability and fear when confronted by Jezebel, who threatened him with death by the next day as retribution for his actions against the prophets of her cherished deity. Consumed by fear and overwhelmed by the circumstances, he made the decision to flee for his life, leaving his loyal servant behind and venturing into the desolate wilderness. Elijah's actions serve as a poignant reminder of how many of us allow anxiety to govern our lives. In doing so, we often overlook the presence of a friendly higher power ready to intervene with strength and authority when called upon. We take things into our hands only to realize that we are not always equipped to handle them effectively. Ironically, Elijah's fearful flight led him to the very place where God often leads us when we fail to grasp an important lesson: the desert. This barren and solitary setting becomes a metaphorical drawing board, a place of reflection and transformation where we are confronted with our vulnerabilities and where God seeks to mold us anew.

Elijah reached a point of exhaustion and weariness in his role as a prophet. He grew tired of having to suppress his own emotions and desires to align with God's will. The pressure to "fake it until he made it" became burdensome. In that moment, he confronted his own feelings of inadequacy and saw himself as a sad and insufficient individual. He carried a sense of guilt for his inability to trust the same God who had just demonstrated His power through the miraculous fire from heaven. Therefore, he pleaded to be released from his responsibilities without delay and without any possibility of return. Elijah's emotional state suggests that he may have battled with depression, a condition that made him doubt his significance and question his own worth. As a prophet of God, he grappled with the paradox of his own struggles, struggling to find the trust and faith in God that his role demanded. How could he fulfill his calling as a spokesperson for the Divine when he himself couldn't fully trust in the very God he served? Why did have to be in these shoes? Why him? In various aspects of our lives, whether in our professions, ministries, marriages, or as parents, we encounter weariness that can be overwhelming. We reach a point where we long for relief and, in moments of extreme fatigue, may even find ourselves wishing for an end to our struggles.

How does the God of heaven react to this profound demonstration of human frailty? Does He deliver an uplifting message about our significance to Him and the value of life? Or does He confront us with a stern rebuke, revealing His disappointment in our longing for death despite His constant presence with us? No, He sends an angel to give us…food. Yes. Food. An angel roused Elijah from his slumber and instructed him to partake in a divine meal consisting of cake and water, specifically prepared in a heavenly kitchen to cater to Elijah's unique requirements. This nourishment was intended to equip Elijah for an unforeseen journey that lay ahead, of which he had no prior knowledge. While Elijah's sustenance was in the form of physical food, in our own lives, it can take various metaphorical forms. It could manifest as discovering a supportive community, finding a new church that resonates with our beliefs, forming deep connections with friends or family, experiencing the joy of parenthood, uncovering a God-given purpose, or encountering a profound revelation of God Himself. In my personal journey, it was indeed the latter, as the revelation of God Himself became my true sustenance.

I would like to emphasize that God has a profound intentionality in providing precisely what we need during the most challenging moments of our lives, when we wish to be freed from our misery. He does not overlook the very request we believe would alleviate our suffering; instead, He presents something of such magnitude that we would even forget we made that specific request. Upon discovering the greatness of God and His profound presence, my longing to make a permanent escape gradually diminished. Instead, I yearned to encounter Him and accept His love for me. Although I still encountered challenges and wrestled with the complexities of life, God consistently reassured me of His immense power, surpassing any pain or hardship I faced.

When we find ourselves exhausted and weary, even to the point of questioning our own existence, it is important to remember that God is not indifferent to our struggles. Instead, He is deeply concerned about the strength and resilience we need for the journey ahead. In fact, it is often during our moments of deepest discouragement that we find ourselves entrusted with the greatest missions to carry. It is in those times of weakness that God's power and grace can shine through us, allowing us to accomplish remarkable things despite our weariness. So, let us find comfort in knowing that God equips us with the necessary strength to face each day and fulfill the purpose He has for us, even when we feel tired and overwhelmed.

The food Elijah's ate gave him enough strength to walk 40 days and 40 nights until he reached the mountain of God, so He may speak directly to him. How similar it is with the same amount of time Jesus spent in the desert without ingesting anything. Forty is a significant number in biblical symbolism, often representing a period of testing, preparation, or transition. In this context, it signifies the time of solitude and reflection that Elijah needed to experience in order to be renewed and refocused in his faith and calling. Horeb, also known as Mount Sinai, holds great significance in biblical history as the place where Moses encountered God and received the Ten Commandments. By leading Elijah to this sacred mountain, God invites him into a place of divine encounter and revelation.

It's thus impossible to come face to face with God without previously experiencing the darkness of our own existence. It's true that God is surrounded by light in His dwelling place, but He sure loves darkness. For it is sometimes necessary that in order for His marvelous light to shine in our lives and remain lit, we must have gone through perfect darkness. He is right there in our darkest elucubrations, even the very ones riddled with suicidal ideation because he delights in our conception of the irreversible. All He wants is that we surrender for just a moment, so He can show us what He is capable of. In the same way that His own spirit hovered over the waters of a desolate world yet to be formed, His presence permeates the minds that have lost all hope. The enemy's most pervasive lie, whispered through our thoughts in these dark moments, is that God is distant and indifferent. Believing those lies has cost the lives of many. However, it is precisely during these times that He is most intimately connected to us, more than ever before!

The Power of Light over Darkness

From the pits of our darkest contemplations,

Where thoughts entwined with despair's tribulations,

Even amid whispers of ideations dire,

God's presence lingers, fueling His fire.

For He takes delight in our boundless imagination,

Even when consumed by thoughts of devastation,

Yearning to showcase His power and might,

To unveil wondrous miracles in our bleakest night.

With a gentle plea, He beckons us to surrender,

To release our burdens, let His beautiful love render,

For in that fleeting moment of letting go,

He reveals wonders only He can bestow.

Just as His spirit once hovered over the deep,
Creating a world from chaos in a majestic sweep,
So too does He permeate our shattered minds,
Infusing hope and peace where despair binds.

Beware the enemy's lies, cunning and sly,
Whispering distance, indifference with each cry,
For lives have been lost, believing the deceit,
But know, God's presence is near, ever complete.

In the depths of despair, His love is profound,
A solace, a lifeline, where healing is found,
Embrace the truth, let faith be your guide,
For in the darkest moments, God stands beside.

So, when despair threatens to claim your soul,
Remember, His presence makes you whole,
For He is there, intimately connected, and true,
Ready to unveil miracles, just for you.

22. A Still Small Voice

Then He said, "Go out, and stand on the mountain before the Lord." And behold, the Lord passed by, and a great and strong wind tore into the mountains and broke the rocks in pieces before the Lord, but the Lord was not in the wind; and after the wind an earthquake, but the Lord was not in the earthquake; and after the earthquake a fire, but the Lord was not in the fire; and after the fire a still small voice. **1 Kings 19:11-12**

Speaking softly promotes effective communication. When we lower our voice and speak calmly, it encourages the listener to pay closer attention and engage in active listening. It creates a conducive environment for understanding, as it allows the listener to process the message without feeling overwhelmed or defensive. This is the way God chose to engage with Elijah.

The glory of the Lord was found in the still small voice to demonstrate His presence and power in a subtle and gentle manner. Elijah had just experienced a powerful display of God's might through wind, earthquake, and fire, but God was not in any of these dramatic manifestations. Instead, He revealed Himself in a whisper or a still small voice. This choice of communication showcased the depth of God's transcendence and His ability to reveal Himself in unexpected ways. The contrast between the grandeur of natural forces and the quiet whisper highlighted the personal and intimate nature of God's presence. It conveyed the message that God's power and glory are not solely confined to overt displays or sensational events but can also be experienced in the quiet moments of reflection, inner peace, and humble listening.

By appearing in the still small voice, God emphasized the importance of attentive and receptive hearts to truly discern His presence. It also demonstrated His willingness to meet us in our quietest and most vulnerable states, comforting and guiding us with His gentle voice. Ultimately, the glory of the Lord being found in the still small voice invites us to cultivate a spirit of attentiveness, humility, and sensitivity to God's subtle and gentle workings in our lives.

Furthermore, the still small voice reveals God's compassionate and tender nature. Take a moment to imagine yourself in Elijah's position. After experiencing a remarkable victory where God clearly revealed His divine power, you suddenly find yourself fleeing for your life. Overwhelmed by distress, you reach a point where you no longer desire to live and even question your calling as a prophet. It is at this precise moment that Elijah realizes he doesn't require the forceful manifestations of wind, earthquake, or fire. Had God revealed Himself through these powerful elements, it would have further burdened Elijah's fragile state. Instead, what Elijah truly needed was the soothing assurance of God's presence.

Recognizing Elijah's needs, God chose to meet him in a gentle and comforting manner. Despite His immense power and authority, He chooses to communicate with His servant Elijah in a gentle and patient manner. This signifies His desire to connect with us on a personal and intimate level. It reminds us that God is not distant or aloof, but rather intimately involved in our lives, speaking to us with a voice of love, reassurance, and guidance.

In a world filled with noise, distractions, and chaos, this passage calls us to cultivate a spirit of silence, attentiveness, and receptivity. It invites us to create space in our lives to listen for the whisper of God, to seek His presence in the stillness, and to heed His voice even amidst the clamor of life. It teaches us that the glory of the Lord can be found in the seemingly insignificant and quiet moments, reminding us of His constant presence and the depth of His love and care for His people.

Sweet Nothings

From the hush of the night, a whisper so low,
God's still small voice, gentle and slow.
Amidst the chaos and clamor of life's noisy race,
He speaks in the Quiet, revealing His grace.

No thunderous roar or tempest's might,
But a soft murmur, calming the fright.
A soft and tender breeze, a beautiful and tranquil song,
God's still small voice, where the Price of Peace belongs.

In the depths of our souls, He gently speaks,
With words of comfort, for the weary seeks.
In the silent moments, His presence draws near,
Whispering hope, casting away every fear.

Through the storms that rage and winds that blow,
His voice pierces through, like a candle's glow.
It guides and directs, in paths unknown,
With wisdom profound, seeds of truth sown.

His still small voice, a balm for the soul,
Restoring, healing, making brokenness whole.
In the quietude, His love is made known,
A sacred connection, uniquely our own.

So, let us listen in the silence profound,

To the whispers of God, a gentle sound.

For in His still small voice, we find peace,

A divine embrace that will never cease.

Yours Truly

And there came a voice from above the expanse that was over their heads; whenever they stood still, they dropped their wings. --- **Ezekiel 1:25**

23. A Heart Easily Touched by Prayer

Go back and tell Hezekiah, the leader of my people, `This is what the LORD, the God of your father David, says: I have heard your prayer and seen your tears; I will heal you. On the third day from now you will go up to the temple of the LORD. **2 Kings 20:5**

2 Kings 20 recounts a significant event in the life of King Hezekiah of Judah. The chapter begins with Hezekiah falling ill and receiving a message from the prophet Isaiah that he would not recover but die from his illness. Deeply distressed by this news, Hezekiah turns to the Lord in prayer, reminding God of his faithfulness and devotion. Moved by Hezekiah's plea, God sends Isaiah back to the king with a message of healing, promising to add fifteen years to his life.

I personally love this passage because it highlights several important themes and lessons. Firstly, it portrays the power of prayer and the faithfulness of God to respond to the cries of His people. Hezekiah's fervent prayer and his unwavering trust in God's mercy and compassion moved the heart of the Lord, resulting in a miraculous extension of his life. When we approach God with sincere and heartfelt prayers, appealing to His mercy and grace, He will never remain indifferent. Our cries for help, forgiveness, or intervention touch Him. He is compassionate and loving, and He desires to respond to our needs and concerns.

Secondly, it illustrates the sovereignty of God over life and death. Initially, Isaiah's prophecy declared that Hezekiah's illness would be terminal. However, God's response to Hezekiah's prayer demonstrates His authority to alter the course of events according to His divine will. This serves as a reminder that God's plans and timing may surpass human understanding, and His mercy can intervene even in the face of apparent hopelessness.

Additionally, this passage emphasizes the importance of humility and repentance. After being healed, Hezekiah is visited by envoys from Babylon who come to inquire about the sign of his healing. Instead of using this opportunity to testify to the greatness and faithfulness of God, Hezekiah flaunts his wealth and achievements before them, which displeases the Lord. Isaiah delivers a sobering message, foretelling the Babylonian captivity and the loss of Judah's treasures due to Hezekiah's actions. This serves as a cautionary reminder of the consequences of pride and the need for humility and gratitude in our relationship with God.

Ultimately, 2 Kings 20 presents a complex narrative of God's mercy, human faithfulness, and the consequences of our actions. It encourages us to turn to God in times of distress, to trust in His sovereignty, and to walk in humility and obedience before Him. It also reminds us that God's grace and mercy can transform our circumstances, and His plans extend far beyond our limited understanding.

However, it is important to note that God's response may not always align with our expectations or desires. He, in His infinite wisdom, knows what is best for us and may choose to answer our prayers in ways that we may not understand now. His plans are higher than ours, and He sees the bigger picture.

Therefore, when we fervently appeal to God's mercy, it is essential to approach Him with a surrendered heart, trusting that He will respond according to His perfect wisdom and love. We can find comfort and assurance in knowing that God is attentive to our cries and that He will always act in our best interest.

The 2 Kings 20 Poem

From the Kingdom of Judah, a sick king in is dismay,
His name was Hezekiah, seeking a way.
Afflicted by illness, his spirit was weak,
He turned to the Lord; with a prayer he would speak.

"Remember, O Lord, how I've walked in Your ways,
With a heart so loyal, I'm seeking Your praise.
Extend my days, Lord, let me live on,
Restore my health, let Your healing be known."

The prophet Isaiah, a message did bring,
From the Lord Almighty, a comforting wing.
"Go and tell Hezekiah, the ailing king,
I've heard his prayer, and healing I bring."

In three days' time, a sign would appear,
A reassurance that God's promise was near.
The sundial of Ahaz, a shadow would go back,
A miraculous sign, a faith-strengthening track.

The Lord fulfilled His word, as He had said,
Hezekiah was healed, He was no longer in dread.
His faith was rewarded, his life was prolonged,
A testament to the power of God, mighty strong.

In 2 Kings 20:5, we see a tale,
Of a king's plea and God's merciful hail.
A reminder to us, in our times of need,
To turn to the Lord, in faith we should plead.

For He is our healer, our source of relief,
With His loving touch, He mends every grief.
In moments of darkness, His light will guide,
His grace and compassion will forever abide.

So let us remember the story so true,
Of Hezekiah's prayer and the miracle through.

In times of trouble, let us seek God's embrace,
Knowing His mercy will never be erased.
Yours Truly

He shall call upon Me, and I will answer him.
I will be with him in trouble.
I will deliver him and honor him. --- **Psalm 91:15**

24. A Know-it-all God

Even before there is a word on my tongue,
Behold, O Lord, You know it all. **Psalm 139:4**

The omniscience of God is a profound and awe-inspiring attribute that defines His limitless knowledge and understanding. It encompasses His perfect awareness of all things past, present, and future. In His omniscience, God possesses complete knowledge of every detail and intricacy of the universe, from the tiniest particles to the grandest cosmic events.

I am fascinated by hummingbirds. In their creation we witness the exquisite design and artistry of God. Every aspect of their existence reflects the careful craftsmanship of the divine Creator. From their vibrant plumage to their unique flight abilities, hummingbirds display a beauty and functionality that leaves me in awe. Their diminutive size and delicate structure are marvels of engineering. Their compact bodies, lightweight bones, and slender beaks are perfectly suited for their nectar-feeding lifestyle. The intricate details of their feathers, with iridescent colors that shimmer in the sunlight, reveal a level of craftsmanship that surpasses human imagination. The remarkable flight capabilities of hummingbirds testify to God's ingenuity. Their ability to hover in mid-air, fly in any direction, and even perform acrobatic feats is a testament to the divine wisdom embedded within their design.

Unlike human knowledge, which is limited and finite, God's omniscience knows no bounds. He comprehends the depths of every thought, the motives behind every action, and the hidden mysteries that elude human understanding. His wisdom surpasses the wisdom of all creation, for He is the source and sustainer of all knowledge. God's omniscience extends beyond mere awareness of facts and information. It encompasses His understanding of the inner workings of every individual, the complexities of human nature, and the depths of our emotions. He discerns our joys and sorrows, our hopes and fears, and even the unspoken desires of our hearts. Nothing escapes His omniscient gaze.

The implications of God's omniscience are profound. It means that He is never taken by surprise, caught off guard, or unaware of any situation. He sees every event unfold in perfect clarity, perceiving the interconnectedness of all things. His knowledge is not limited by time or space but encompasses the entirety of existence in a timeless and comprehensive manner.

This divine attribute brings me great comfort and reassurance. It assures me that God is intimately acquainted with my life, my struggles, and my needs. He understands the complexities of our circumstances and offers guidance and wisdom accordingly. In His omniscience, He is aware of the path that lies before us, leading us towards His perfect purposes.

Yet, God's omniscience also serves as a reminder of His holiness and righteousness. He sees every act of injustice, every violation of His commands, and every thought that falls short of His standards. His omniscience highlights the need for repentance, forgiveness, and alignment with His will.

As we contemplate the omniscience of God, we are humbled by the vastness of His understanding and the depths of His wisdom. It invites us to approach Him with reverence and awe, knowing that He sees and knows all. It encourages us to seek His guidance, trust in His providence, and surrender to His infinite knowledge.

He counts the number of the stars.

He gives names to all of them.--- **Psalm 147:4**

A Poem to Perfect Knowledge

Across the galaxies where mysteries lie,

Resides the wisdom that transcends the sky.

A knowledge boundless, unfathomably deep,

Where all things past, present, and future, God keeps.

Omniscient Creator, with eyes that perceive,
Every hidden thought, every heart's reprieve.
No secret escapes His omniscient gaze,
For He knows all things, in endless arrays.

He knows the stars that dance in cosmic delight,
Their radiant paths, their patterns of light.
He knows the oceans, their depths and their tides,
The creatures within, where their secrets reside.

From the dawn of creation to the end of all days,
His omniscience guides, in wondrous displays.
He sees every sparrow that takes to the sky,
Counts every hair, as they fall and lie.

He knows the intricate workings of cells,
The mysteries of life, where the miracle dwells.
He knows the intentions behind every deed,
The whispers of hearts, the desires we need.

In the rolling of time, His knowledge we find,
Every thread woven, intricately aligned.
No question too complex, no puzzle too vast,
For in His vast wisdon, understanding is cast.

Yet, His knowledge goes beyond the realms we know,
For He sees the depths where our souls ebb and flow.
He knows our struggles, our joys, and our fears,
And offers compassion to wipe away tears.

In His omniscience, there is comfort and grace,

For He knows our weaknesses, our sins to erase.
He guides us with love, with wisdom untold,
In His omniscience, our worries unfold.

As I marvel at the Beautiful and Omniscient One,
Whose knowledge encompasses all under the sun.
In His wisdom, I will find comfort and rest,
For God's intelligence knows what is best.

In the vast sweep of His omniscient view,
I will cuddle in His bosom, knowing His love is true.
For He knows us intimately, deep within,
And in His vast knowledge, our lives begin.

Go on and try His all-knowing embrace,
And trust in His wisdom, in every place.
For in His omniscience, we find peace,
Knowing He holds all knowledge, without cease.
Yours Truly

25. "So, you think you can God?"

Where is the way to the dwelling of light?
And darkness, where is its place,
That you may take it to its territory,
That you may know the paths to its home?
Do you know it, because you were born then,
because the number of your days is great? **Job 38: 19-21**

It is truly captivating when a teenager confidently asserts that they have a better understanding of life than their parents. This teenager possesses a self-assured demeanor, firmly believing that their knowledge and comprehension surpass that of their parents. They express their beliefs and opinions with confidence, often asserting them assertively during discussions and disagreements with their parents. This teenager may also tend to challenge their parents' authority and question their decisions, relying on their own perceived wisdom. In some cases, they heavily rely on technology and digital platforms to support their arguments, using online resources and social media platforms to gather information and reinforce their claims.

When contemplating this dynamic, one cannot help but wonder what thoughts cross the minds of the parents, reflecting on the day their child was born—fragile, helpless, and entirely dependent on them. The parents may experience a flood of emotions as they recall the early stages of their child's life and the immense care they provided. Similarly, it is conceivable that God may experience similar sentiments when we attempt to challenge His wisdom. Where were we when He one day decided to be God?

God breaks His silence and addresses Job directly. The chapter opens with a series of rhetorical questions, emphasizing God's vast knowledge and authority over the universe. God asks Job where he was when the foundations of the earth were laid, when the morning stars sang together, and when the sea was given its boundaries. Through these questions, God highlights His power and supremacy as the Creator of all things. He also put Job in his place as a mortal and finite human being.

Job's reflections prompted a response from God, who presented a series of satirical and thought-provoking questions. Through these inquiries, God sought to humble Job, highlighting his limited understanding, and challenging his wounded sense of dignity.

Challenging the purpose and workings of God is audacious, as it attempts to equate our intellect with His. Attempting to place our intellect on par with God's is to diminish His sovereignty and elevate ourselves to a level that we cannot attain. It reflects a lack of humility and a failure to recognize the vast difference between our limited understanding and God's omniscience. It is a futile endeavor that only leads to pride and a distorted perspective. It is in recognizing our finite nature and embracing our dependence on God's wisdom that we can truly grow in understanding and humility.

God's character is continually revealed through His intimate involvement in the intricate workings of the natural world. In awe-inspiring displays, He showcases His authority and power over the elements, unveiling the depths of His wisdom and care for His creation. As the morning dawns upon the Earth, it is not by mere chance or random occurrence. God, in His sovereignty, commands the sun to rise, painting the sky with vibrant hues, and orchestrating the transition from darkness to light. This daily phenomenon reflects His control over time and His precise design for the rhythms of life.

In the depths of the sea, where mysteries abound, God asserts His dominion. The vast expanses of the ocean, with their unfathomable depths and diverse ecosystems, stand as a testament to His creative mastery. From the smallest marine organisms to the majestic creatures that inhabit its waters, every living being reflects His intricate design and providential care. God's authority extends beyond the seas to the atmospheric realm. He governs the storehouses of snow and hail, crafting each snowflake and orchestrating the descent of frozen precipitation. The delicate beauty of snowflakes and the power of hailstorms both bear witness to His meticulous attention to detail and His ability to bring forth beauty and purpose even from seemingly harsh elements. In the skies above, God commands the paths of lightning, illuminating the heavens with its brilliant flashes. This captivating display of electrical energy showcases His control over the forces of nature and reminds us of His awe-inspiring might.

Through these vivid depictions, God reveals His profound understanding and meticulous control over creation. He showcases His intentionality and attentive care for every aspect of the natural world. From the grandeur of the cosmos to the tiniest intricate details of life, His fingerprints are evident everywhere. It is through His creation that we catch a glimpse of His divine character, and we are reminded of His enduring love and providential guidance in our lives.

The meticulous monitoring of natural elements by God serves as a powerful reminder of His intimate knowledge and care for our needs and desires. If He attends to every detail of the natural world, how much more intimately does He know and understand the intricacies of our lives? This realization invites us to ponder the depth of His love and involvement in our individual journeys.

In moments of pain and darkness, the psalmist in **Psalms 89-90** provides us with a profound lesson. It is during these challenging times that we have the capacity to remember and reflect on the works, character, and promises of God. By intentionally recalling His faithfulness throughout our lives, we gain perspective and find solace in knowing that He has been with us every step of the way. Within the psalms, we encounter a profound truth—that "crying out" to God is not an admission of weak faith, but rather an act of trust. It is a heartfelt expression of our reliance on Him, knowing that He hears our cries and will respond according to His perfect timing and wisdom. In our vulnerability and pain, we find comfort in knowing that we can pour out our hearts to the One who deeply understands us and cares for us.

As we reflect on the psalmist's words, we are encouraged to embrace the power of remembrance and reflection. By intentionally recollecting the ways in which God has proven Himself trustworthy in the past, we are fortified in our faith and equipped to face the trials and uncertainties of the present. These moments of recollection serve as pillars of hope, reminding us that God's faithfulness endures even in the darkest of times. In the midst of pain and adversity, let us take solace in the truth that God's knowledge, love, and faithfulness extend far beyond our comprehension.

Answer Me

In chambers unseen, where darkness abides,
A realm beyond mortal's feeble strides,
The storehouses of snow, a mystery untold,
Where secrets of winter's beauty unfold.

"Who has birthed the ice?" the voice proclaims,
And forged the frost in its intricate frames?
Its crystals of wonder, glistening bright,
Blanketing the earth in a shimmering white.

From the womb of the storm, hailstones descend,
As nature's percussion, a message to send.
"Have you beheld the treasures of hail?
Fashioned by the Master Weaver, amidst the gale."

An arsenal of frozen might, fearsome and grand,
Held captive by God's mighty hand,
From the vaults of heaven, they are hurled,
A testament to His dominion unfurled.

Oh, mortal soul, humble in your quest,
To fathom the wonders by which you are blessed,

Bow before the Creator, in awe and adoration,
For His majesty is beyond your comprehension.

In Job's tale of trials, in anguish he wept,
Yet God's voice from the whirlwind, softly crept,
A reminder of His power, His presence so near,
To trust in His wisdom, banishing all fear.

Let us heed these words, in awe and respect,
Embrace the mysteries that we cannot dissect,
For in the cords of life, His hand weaves,
And in His divine plan, our faith receives.

So, marvel at the wonders in every creation,
Embrace the divine in humble contemplation,
For in Job's encounter, wisdom did unfold,
God's voice in the storm, a story to be told.
Yours Truly

Lift up your heads, O gates! And be lifted up, O ancient doors, that the King of glory may come in. Who is this King of glory? The Lord, strong and mighty, the Lord, mighty in battle! -- **Psalm 24:7-8**

26. Not Pressed by Time

The least of you will become a thousand, the smallest of a mighty nation. I am the Lord. in its time I will do this swiftly **Isaiah 60:22**

Waiting for personal or professional opportunities can be an agonizing experience. It involves anticipating significant life events or milestones, like waiting to receive college acceptance letters, job offers, or promotion decisions. The uncertainty and anticipation surrounding these opportunities can take a toll on one's mental and emotional well-being. The waiting period often triggers impatience, frustration, and anxiety as individuals eagerly await the outcome and the potential impact it will have on their lives.

People generally dislike waiting due to several reasons. Firstly, waiting can be perceived as a waste of time, especially in a fast-paced society where efficiency and productivity are highly valued. It can feel frustrating to have to delay or postpone one's plans or activities.

Secondly, waiting can trigger feelings of impatience and restlessness. The desire for immediate gratification and instant results has become more prevalent in today's culture. Waiting challenges this expectation and can lead to feelings of discomfort and dissatisfaction.

Additionally, waiting can evoke a sense of uncertainty and lack of control. Not knowing how long the wait will last or what the outcome will be, can be anxiety-inducing. Humans generally prefer certainty and control over their circumstances, and waiting undermines these desires.

Lastly, the availability of modern technology and conveniences has reduced people's tolerance for waiting. With instant access to information, fast communication, and on-demand services, waiting for even a short period can feel inconvenient and undesirable.

Overall, people dislike waiting because it disrupts their plans, triggers impatience, evokes uncertainty, and challenges their desire for immediate results and control.

Patience can be a difficult virtue to cultivate, especially when we are eagerly waiting for something, particularly when it involves waiting on God. It is human nature to desire certainty and control, and waiting for something without a clear timeline can be incredibly challenging. Waiting for God's timing can be unsettling. We often find comfort in having a set schedule or a planned timeline. It's as if we want God to mark the date on our calendars or provide us with a tracking number to monitor the progress of His plans. But the reality is that God's ways are higher than ours, and His timing is perfect.

When God decides to move, He does so swiftly and decisively. However, the exact moment of His movement may remain unknown to us. It requires faith and trust to wait patiently, knowing that God will act at the right time. We may struggle with the uncertainty and impatience, but we can find solace in the knowledge that God is fully aware of our circumstances and has a purpose for the waiting.

Isaiah 60:22 reminds us of the incredible potential and possibilities that exist when we put our trust in the Lord. It encourages us to embrace our journey, even when it involves waiting, knowing that

God's promises are sure, and He will bring them to pass in His perfect and swift timing.

Wait on the LORD; Be of good courage, And He shall strengthen your heart; Wait, I say, on the LORD! --- **Psalms 27:14**

Beautiful Patience

In the movement of the waiting hour,
Where hope meets uncertainty's power,
I find myself in patient surrender,
Trusting in God's timing so tender.

With every passing day and night,
I seek His guidance, His holy light,
For in this waiting, I learn to be,
To let go of control and simply see.

Like a seed buried deep in the ground,
I await His touch, His voice profound,
For in the silence, His whispers I hear,
Guiding me closer, dispelling my fear.

Oh, waiting on God, a sacred dance,
Where faith and trust find their chance,
To bloom amidst the darkest hour,
And witness His mighty, loving power.

Though days may stretch, and nights may seem long,
In this waiting, I grow ever strong,
For His plans, like a masterpiece divine,
Unfold in moments that are truly sublime.

In the waiting, my soul finds rest,

Nurtured by His grace, I am blessed,
For His timing is perfect, His ways so true,
In His presence, all things are made anew.

So I wait with hope, with steadfast heart,
Knowing that every moment is a precious part,
Of the journey that leads me closer to Him,
In the waiting, my faith grows, bright and prim.

For in the waiting, I find His embrace,
His love, His peace, His endless grace,
And when the time is right, He'll make it known,
In His perfect timing, my purpose will be shown.

So I wait with open hands and open heart,
Trusting in His plan, though it may start,
With uncertainty and trials to bear,
In the waiting, I find strength to dare.

For waiting on God is a sacred art,
A journey that molds and shapes my heart,
In patience and surrender, I come to find,
That His promises endure, forever kind.

So, I embrace the waiting, with gratitude,
For in this process, I am renewed,
And as I wait on God, my soul's delight,
I know His plans will unfold, shining bright.
Yours Truly

27. An Unchanging God

"For I am the LORD, I do not change; Therefore, you are not consumed, O sons of Jacob. **Malachi 3:6-10**

Many individuals find it challenging to commit to reading the Bible in its entirety. They may start from the beginning and make progress through books like Genesis, Exodus, and even part of Leviticus. However, as they delve deeper into the text, they encounter accounts that evoke shock and surprise. For instance, the story of the Great Flood reveals that only eight individuals survived while the rest of humanity and animals perished. Similarly, the firstborn in Egypt, regardless of their social status, were executed if their households lacked the protective blood on their doorposts. Jericho, apart from a prostitute and her family, was annihilated entirely, sparing no human or animal. Even simply gathering wood on the Sabbath led to a man being stoned to death, and two sons of the High Priest faced the wrath of God through consuming fire for failing to adhere to prescribed worship practices.

Reading through the Old Testament can be daunting due to such narratives. The God depicted in these scriptures is described as a consuming fire and a jealous God. It raises questions about how one can embrace such a deity, let alone having a relationship with Him. The psalmist further emphasizes this perception by stating that God hates all who do wrong. Considering these portrayals, individuals may be inclined to avoid delving into the entire book.

As a result, some people jump to the New Testament and begin reading the Gospels of Matthew, Mark, Luke, and John. These accounts present a different side of God. Jesus, the central figure, exemplifies compassion by embracing children and blessing infants. He miraculously feeds the hungry, fills boats with fish, and raises the dead to life. Jesus dines with societal outcasts, forgives those entangled in scandal, and extends friendship to despised tax collectors. Everyone is familiar with Jesus' teaching to love one's enemies.

However, despite the apparent contrast in the depiction of God between the two testaments, it is important to remember that both testaments are expressions of the same Lord God. In the Old Testament, God intervenes on behalf of Israel, the chosen nation entrusted with preserving His word and fulfilling His promises. God acts zealously to protect His plan of salvation by defeating Israel's enemies, who posed a threat to that plan. Specific commands were given to use force against unbelievers who obstructed God's purpose. Yet, with the birth of Jesus, the Savior, and the completion of God's salvation plan, the nation of Israel no longer played its unique role.

Moreover, attentive readers of the Bible will discern the consistency in the character of the Lord God throughout both testaments. Both portray God as a condemner and a forgiver, a God of wrath and a God of love. The Old Testament reveals a loving God who graciously provides for an undeserving nation by supplying water, manna, and quail. God's grace persists in the face of human unfaithfulness. Similarly, the New Testament reaffirms God's justice, stating that those who do not believe will face condemnation. Jesus Himself affirmed the significance of the Old Testament scriptures and did not come to abolish them but to fulfill them (**Matthew 5:17**). The New Testament builds upon the foundation of the Old Testament, providing further understanding and fulfillment of God's promises and purposes. Furthermore, Jesus Himself claimed to be one with the Father, stating, "I and the Father are one" (**John 10:30**). He also declared that whoever has seen Him has seen the Father (**John 14:9**). This indicates the essential unity and identity of Jesus with God the Father.

The Scriptures proclaim an unchanging Lord God. He reveals Himself as a holy and just God who punishes all sin, while simultaneously manifesting Himself as a loving God who sends a Substitute, Jesus Christ, to bear the punishment in our place. In the Old Testament book of Isaiah, Chapter 53, we encounter the prophecy of Christ's suffering for our transgressions and iniquities, bringing us peace and healing. The contrast between the Old and New Testaments highlights the progressive revelation of God's character and plan of salvation throughout history. It reveals the unfolding story of God's love and mercy, culminating in the person and work of Jesus Christ. Both testaments ultimately point to the same God who is consistent and unchanging in His nature, displaying a harmonious unity despite the apparent differences in presentation.

The Bible's overarching message revolves around the law and the gospel. The law exposes our sins, while the gospel presents the good news of our Savior from sin, Jesus the Messiah. Consequently, we rejoice in the unchanging proclamation that the wages of sin lead to death, but through God's gift, we receive eternal life in Christ Jesus our Lord.

Jesus Christ is the same yesterday and today and forever. -- **Hebrews 13:8**

The Same God

In ancient pages, a tale unfolds,
The Bible's story, the truths it holds.
From Genesis to Exodus, we embark,
Through Leviticus, a challenging arc.

But wait, what's this? A flood so great,
Only eight souls, sealed by fate.
The firstborn of Egypt met their demise,
Without blood on the door, no one survives.

Jericho trembled, fell to the ground,
Except for Rahab, who refuge found.
A man gathering wood on the Sabbath day,
Stoned to death, God's law held sway.

The High Priest's sons, with misguided fire,
Faced divine wrath, a consequence dire.
These tales of old, they test our hearts,
As we question the ways God imparts.

In the Old Testament, a vengeful view,
A consuming fire, a jealousy true.
How can we embrace such a fearsome guide,
A God who hates those who go astride?

But in the New Testament, a different sight,
Jesus, the Savior, shining with light.
He embraced children, blessed the weak,
Fed the hungry, comforted the meek.

He raised the dead, performed miracles bold,
Dined with outcasts, their stories told.
Love your enemies, His words so clear,

A message of hope, dispelling fear.

Yet let us not forget, as we explore,
That both testaments from one God pour.
In the Old, Israel, a chosen nation,
Protected by God, fulfilling salvation.

But with the birth of Christ, a wondrous plan,
The role of Israel transformed by God's hand.
Consistency lies in God's character divine,
A condemner, a forgiver, both intertwine.

In grace, the Old Testament reveals,
God's constant love, His faithfulness seals.
The New Testament, too, echoes the same,
Condemnation for those who reject His name.

The Scriptures proclaim, unchanging and true,
God's justice, His mercy, in vibrant hue.
Isaiah's prophecy, a suffering foretold,
By His wounds, our healing, so manifold.

Reconciliation, through Christ's sacrifice,
Our sins forgiven; God's love does entice.
Law and gospel, a message so grand,
Sin's wages are death, but hope is at hand.

So, in these ancient texts, we find our way,
Guided by God, in every word we say.
Let faith embrace the unchanging plan,
The gift of eternal life in God's own span.
Yours Truly

Made in United States
Orlando, FL
20 June 2023